BEST OF THE BEST PRESENTS

DEEP SUTH DISH

Mama's Grilled and Smothered Chicken, page 124

BEST OF THE BEST PRESENTS

DEEP SOUTH DISH

Homestyle Southern Recipes

Mary Foreman

QUAIL RIDGE PRESS
Preserving America's Food Heritage

ISBN 978-1-938879-13-5

Manufactured in the United States of America
by CJK Print Possibilities
First printing April 2015 • Second, May 2015 • Third, July 2015
Fourth, October 2015 • Fifth, December 2015

Photographs by Mary Foreman, except:
Food styling and photographs by Christian and Elise Stella,
pages 2, 15, 43, 63, 83, 121, 129, 153, 179, and 189
Photograph by James Stefiuk, page 159
Photographs by Gwen McKee, pages 25, 40, 50, 132, 133, and 209

On the back cover: Shrimp Creole, page 152, Classic Southern Tomato
Pie, page 92; Perfect Southern Fried Chicken, page 128

Significant discounts for bulk sales are available. Please contact Quail Ridge Press at
1-800-343-1583 or info@quailridge.com.

QUAIL RIDGE PRESS
P. O. Box 123 • Brandon, MS 39043 • 1-800-343-1583
info@quailridge.com • www.quailridge.com

To the family at DeepSouthDish.com and across our social media pages, you are truly responsible for this cookbook. Your continued support, your heartwarming letters, your prayers, your daily friendship, and frankly, your insistence, are what brought this cookbook to fruition. I hope that it is everything that you expected . . . and more.

Real Southern
Cornbread, page 36

Contents

Southern Sweet Tea, page 22

Preface

Hurricane Katrina hit the Mississippi Gulf Coast with a vengeance in 2005. I had lost my parents a few years before, and now, after a legal career that spanned more than 20 years, the corporate law department I had most recently worked with for many of those years was uprooting and relocating out west. I was left with no job, no daily connection and camaraderie with my coworkers, and in its place was the physical and emotional devastation of Katrina that literally surrounded me everywhere I looked. It left me with a certain indescribable loss, emptiness, and loneliness. With a 50th birthday on the horizon, and economic strife across the country, finding comparable work was a difficult task. So I reached deep down inside, searching for what it was I was supposed to do. And it came to me to turn my talents toward something that I truly loved to do. Well, I certainly loved to cook.

One day I was searching the Internet for something, and inadvertently discovered the world of blogs. It seemed people could share what they did well and had an interest in with other people. Aha! I have always loved writing, so this looked like something I could do.

Soon after, I started my own general interest blog, sharing my daily life and experiences, and in that, finding a connection of friendship with others not only in my neighborhood and state, but across the world. It was enjoyable and something I felt very comfortable sharing.

Being a working mother, I had used shortcut appliances and convenience products like everybody else to get meals on the table, but as I reconnected with the kitchen, creating and making recipes the way my mother and grandmother had, I found a certain peace and solace in the process of cooking the old-fashioned way. As I began sharing memories and writing about favorite family recipes and the dinners I was making every day on my blog, I felt comfort in the memories of the emotional connection with my mother and grand-mother. *It was as if they were in the kitchen with me.*

Before long, the recipes and memories began to take on a life of their own. In August of 2009, I founded Deep South Dish, a website dedicated solely to my homespun recipes and writing. Day after day, I began receiving letters from readers who said my website was like sitting down with a friend and reviving shared memories of times in their own loved ones' kitchens while growing up. Many responded how serving a particular one of my dishes brought back mem-ories of favorite tastes from years gone by. One made a recipe for residents of a nursing home that brought smiles and cheers. Others made them for their own parents, reviving wonderful taste memories. Others wrote that as they took the first bite, they were immediately transformed to childhood and being at the table with their beloved grandmother, and the affectionate memories associated with those days. Another wrote how he had reconnected with his own past while bringing Sunday dinners back, helping to teach a foster child the same emotional connection he had had with his own family during those dinners, and creating new ones to anchor his new life.

It was the winds of a hurricane that literally blew the Deep South Dish blog into existence, and as the saying goes, when one door closes, another one opens. Through loss there is often found purpose and redemption. I knew I had found my calling in sharing my memories and my recipes at Deep South Dish.

Today, literally millions of readers visit my blog on a regular basis. And they continue to write, thanking me for the inspiration to return to the kitchen to connect to their own past...for teaching them to cook like their grandmothers... to share their own memories they recalled as they cooked the recipes.... Truly, I have been encouraged never to set my pen down, to continue to share my recipes and my food and my family, along with so many good memories with my blogger friends all over the world.

Mary Foreman

Appetizers & Beverages

Prep time: 10 min

Inactive time: 2 hours

Servings: 4–6

Marinated Blue Crab Fingers

1 pound blue crab fingers (claw tips)

1 cup bottled Italian dressing

½ cup vegetable oil

1 tablespoon red wine vinegar

Juice 1 medium lemon

Couple dashes Worcestershire

1 small rib celery, finely minced

1 tablespoon finely minced garlic

1 teaspoon parsley flakes

¼ teaspoon dried basil

¼ teaspoon kosher salt

¼ teaspoon black pepper

½ teaspoon Old Bay Seasoning

¼ teaspoon Cajun seasoning

1) Place 1 layer of crab claws in a storage container.

2) Whisk together all remaining ingredients, and evenly distribute part of the marinade over claws, repeating layers of claws and marinade.

3) Cover, and refrigerate at least 2 hours.

4) Arrange on a platter before serving.

Cook's Note: You may substitute olive oil; however, use a light olive oil and not a strong extra virgin olive oil.

Prep time:
10 min

Cook time:
20 min

Yield:
About 3 cups

Hot Crab Dip

1 pound crabmeat

2 (8-ounce) blocks cream cheese, softened

1 cup mayonnaise

2 tablespoons grated onion

¼ teaspoon kosher salt

¼ teaspoon black pepper

¼ teaspoon garlic powder

¼ teaspoon Old Bay Seasoning

¼ teaspoon Cajun seasoning (optional)

¼ teaspoon Worcestershire (optional)

⅓ cup heavy cream, more or less

1) Preheat oven to 375°. Butter a 1½-quart casserole dish; set aside.

2) Place crabmeat in a colander to drain, and pick through for any stray shell; set aside.

3) Meanwhile, combine cream cheese with mayonnaise, onion, salt, pepper, garlic powder, Old Bay, Cajun seasoning, and Worcestershire. Add cream a little at a time, using only enough to loosen the dip.

4) Gently fold in crab, and spoon into buttered casserole dish. Bake 20–25 minutes, or until bubbly and heated through, and lightly browned on top.

5) Serve immediately with assorted crackers or toast points.

Prep time: 15 min

Cook Time: none

Servings: 4–6

Roasted Red Pepper Pimento Cheese

- 2 medium-size red bell peppers
- 4 cups shredded sharp Cheddar cheese
- ¼ cup grated Vidalia or other sweet onion
- ½ cup mayonnaise
- ¼ cup buttermilk
- 1 teaspoon Creole mustard
- ¼–½ teaspoon Cajun seasoning (optional)
- ½ teaspoon hot sauce (optional)
- ¼ teaspoon Worcestershire
- Kosher salt and black pepper to taste

ROASTED RED PEPPERS:

1) Place bell peppers under broiler, or place over an open flame, turning until blistered.

2) Transfer to a zippered bag, or set on a plate covered with a clean dish towel to steam for at least 5 minutes.

3) Halve, peeling off skins, discarding any seeds and membrane; slice and dice.

PIMENTO CHEESE:

1) In a large bowl, mix Cheddar cheese, onion, and roasted red peppers.

2) In a separate small bowl, combine mayonnaise, buttermilk, and mustard with all remaining seasonings. Add to cheese mixture, and combine well.

3) Serve immediately or refrigerate. Allow to come to room temperature before serving.

Variation: Use 2½ cups shredded sharp Cheddar cheese with 1 cup shredded Monterey Jack cheese and ½ cup shredded Parmesan cheese.

Prep time:
10 min

Cook time:
20 min

Servings:
About 10

Party Shrimp

SAUCE:

½ cup each: vegetable oil and light olive oil

½ cup beer, wine, broth, or water

¼ cup red wine vinegar

¼ cup chopped red bell pepper

¼ cup thinly sliced green onions

2 teaspoons spicy mustard

1 teaspoon Worcestershire

1 tablespoon sugar

2 teaspoons kosher salt

¼ teaspoon each: black pepper and red pepper flakes

½ teaspoon each: Cajun seasoning, Old Bay Seasoning, and Italian seasoning

½ tablespoon chopped parsley

Juice of ½ lemon

SHRIMP:

1 stick unsalted butter, divided

3 pounds large (30/40-count) unpeeled, headed raw shrimp

½ lemon, sliced

2 large garlic cloves, smashed

Crab boil or seafood seasoning

1) Whisk together Sauce ingredients; set aside.

2) Preheat oven to 350°. Place ½ stick butter in bottom of a 9x13-inch baking dish, and place into oven, just until butter is melted. Slice other ½ stick butter; set aside.

3) Place shrimp into baking dish, and pour Sauce all over; stir. Scatter lemon slices and garlic on top; dot with remaining ½ stick butter.

4) Bake 10 minutes, remove, and stir; return to oven for another 10 minutes or until shrimp is cooked through and no longer translucent.

5) Remove from oven; sprinkle generously with crab boil; stir, and sprinkle again. Let rest in juices until ready to serve.

Prep time:
10 min

Cook time:
1 hour

Servings:
4–6

Deviled Chicken Wings

4 pounds raw chicken wings

1 tablespoon light brown sugar

1 tablespoon paprika

1 teaspoon salt

½ teaspoon black pepper

1 teaspoon Cajun seasoning

½ teaspoon garlic powder

½ teaspoon onion powder

½ stick butter, melted

¼ cup hot sauce

1) Disjoint and separate wings, if desired, reserving wing tips for another use.

2) Blot wings with a paper towel. Combine next 7 ingredients, setting aside ½ tablespoon of seasoning mixture. Layer wings in 3 layers in a covered container, sprinkling seasoning on each layer, and tossing after each application. Cover, and refrigerate for at least 1 hour.

3) Preheat oven to 375°. Line a baking sheet with nonstick aluminum foil, and place an oven safe rack on baking sheet. Spray rack on both sides generously with nonstick spray, and arrange wings on the rack. Bake 20 minutes.

4) Remove wings; increase oven temperature to 425°; sprinkle half of reserved seasoning over wings; return to oven. Bake at 425° 20 minutes longer.

5) Remove, turn, sprinkle with remaining seasoning, and bake 15–20 minutes longer, or until cooked through.

6) Combine melted butter and hot sauce; drizzle over wings, and transfer to platter.

Brown Sugar Candied Bacon

1 pound quality thick-cut regular or applewood bacon

½ cup packed light or dark brown sugar

1 teaspoon spicy dry mustard

2 teaspoons chili powder

¼ teaspoon Cajun seasoning or cayenne pepper

Chopped pecans (optional)

1) Preheat oven to 350°. For easy cleanup, line a jellyroll pan with aluminum foil. Place an oven-safe rack on top, and spray liberally with nonstick spray; set aside.

2) Place brown sugar, dry mustard, chili powder, and Cajun seasoning in a zippered bag; seal, and shake until well mixed. Toss bacon in mixture a few strips at a time, and lay coated bacon strips on rack.

3) If using pecans, shake in the remaining brown sugar mixture after you've coated all bacon, and then sprinkle them on top of bacon. Sprinkle any remaining brown sugar mixture on top of each piece of bacon.

4) Bake 30–45 minutes, until crisp. Let bacon cool on rack, or transfer to a sheet of parchment paper in a single layer.

5) Eat as is for a snack or with a meal; use on sandwiches; crumble over a salad; top homemade vanilla ice cream.

Prep time: 20 min

Cook time: 30 min

Servings: About 24

Potluck & Party Meatballs

MEATBALLS:

1 pound ground beef

½ cup bread crumbs

⅓ cup finely minced onion

¼ cup milk

1 large egg

1 tablespoon fresh parsley

1 teaspoon kosher salt

⅛ teaspoon black pepper

½ teaspoon Worcestershire

¼ cup olive, vegetable oil, or vegetable shortening

SAUCE:

1 (12-ounce) bottle chili sauce, or 1 batch homemade (page 160)

1 (10-ounce) jar grape jelly

1–2 tablespoons hot pepper jelly (optional)

1) Mix ground beef, bread crumbs, onion, milk, egg, parsley, salt, pepper, and Worcestershire. Shape into 1-inch balls.

2) Heat oil in a large skillet, and brown meatballs. Remove Meatballs from skillet, and set aside.

SAUCE:

1) Pour off fat from skillet. Add chili sauce and jellies into skillet, and heat, stirring constantly, until melted. Return Meatballs to skillet, and simmer, uncovered, about 30 minutes.

2) To keep warm, place into a chafing or warming dish, or crockpot, and keep covered on LOW, checking occasionally to make sure Meatballs are not crumbling.

Slow Cooker method: Heat Sauce on stovetop. Place heated Sauce and prepared Meatballs in slow cooker, and cook on HIGH 2 hours, then another hour on LOW.

Variation: Try substituting jellied cranberry sauce or a small bottle of barbecue sauce in place of the grape jelly.

Prep time:
10 min

Cook time:
20 min

Yield:
4 dozen

Spicy Cheese Bites

Couple dashes hot sauce

2 sticks unsalted butter, softened

1 (10-ounce) block cheese
(Cheddar, Swiss, Pepper
Jack, Monterey Jack or any
combination), shredded

2¼ cups cake flour

¼ teaspoon Cajun seasoning

⅛ teaspoon cayenne pepper
(optional)

2½ cups Rice Krispies

1) Preheat oven to 350°. Add hot sauce
to butter, and cream with a mixer; add
shredded cheese, and beat just until
combined.

2) In a separate bowl, sift flour, Cajun
seasoning, and cayenne pepper together.
Stir in Rice Krispies.

3) Add flour mixture to butter mixture about
½ cup at a time, until combined.

4) Break off small pieces (about a teaspoon),
and roll each into a ball. Place on an
ungreased cookie sheet, and bake about 20
minutes, or until lightly browned.

5) Cool slightly on baking sheet, then transfer
to a cooling rack.

Prep time: 10 min

Cook time: 1 hour

Yield: 4–6

Southern Cheese Straws

1 (1-pound) block extra sharp Cheddar cheese, shredded

1 stick unsalted butter

2 cups all-purpose flour, divided

1 teaspoon salt

Dash of black pepper

¼ teaspoon cayenne pepper

Dash of garlic powder

Cook's Note: If you don't have a cookie press, roll dough out ¼ inch thick. Cut into narrow strips, 6 inches in length. Transfer to parchment-lined baking sheet, and twist strips, if desired. Bake as directed.

1) Preheat oven to 325°. Process cheese, butter, 1 cup of flour, salt, black pepper, cayenne, and garlic powder, adding additional flour ¼ cup at a time as needed, until dough begins to gather around the blade. Dough should be pliable enough to pipe through a cookie press.

2) Using the star tip of a cookie press, place a portion of dough in the press and pipe out strips across the length of a piece of parchment paper on an ungreased cookie sheet.

3) Bake 20–25 minutes, or until golden brown and crisp. Cut into 3-inch long strips, and transfer to a cooling rack to cool completely. Store in a tightly covered container.

Prep time: 15 min

Cook time: 6 min

Yield: 1 gallon

Southern Sweet Tea

Simple ingredients—it's the method that makes it southern.

8 cups ice cold water

8 cups boiling water

4 family-size tea bags

1½ cups sugar

Low-Calorie Diet Tea: Use sugar substitute in place of sugar.

1) Fill a gallon pitcher with 8 cups cold water; set aside.

2) Boil remaining 8 cups water, add tea bags, and steep 6 minutes.

3) Lightly squeeze tea bags, remove, and discard.

4) Whisk in sugar until fully dissolved, and set aside to cool to room temperature. Carefully add to cold water; stir.

5) Refrigerate until tea is fully chilled and flavor develops, before serving.

Prep time:
10 min

Inactive time:
8 hours

Servings:
About 6

Old-Fashioned Homemade Lemonade

SIMPLE SYRUP:

½ cup water

1½ cups sugar

LEMONADE:

1½ cups freshly squeezed lemon juice (about 8 lemons)

Zest of 1 lemon

5 cups cold water

Additional sliced lemon, for garnish (optional)

1) Make Simple Syrup by bringing water and sugar to a boil. Boil 3 minutes, stirring regularly, until mixture becomes clear and slightly thickened. Set aside to cool.

2) Add lemon juice to a 2-quart pitcher along with lemon zest and cold water. Whisk in cooled Simple Syrup; refrigerate overnight, or for at least 8 hours.

3) Serve in tall glasses over ice, and garnish with lemon slices, if desired.

Strawberry Lemonade: Clean and wash 1 pint of strawberries; purée in food processor; strain, and add to lemonade.

Prep time:
10 min

Cook time:
none

Servings:
1 or 2

Hurricane Cocktail

A Big Easy favorite!

2 ounces light rum

2 ounces dark rum

2 ounces grenadine

1 ounce Simple Syrup (page 24)

Juice of 2 limes

2 ounces orange juice

Orange wedge, for garnish

Cherries, for garnish

1) Mix all liquids in a cocktail shaker.

2) Pour into a tall hurricane glass half full of crushed ice. Top off with additional ice.

3) Garnish with an orange slice and some cherries.

Prep time: 10 min

Inactive time: Overnight

Servings: 2

Frozen Watermelon Margaritas

1 small to medium watermelon
½ cup silver tequila
¼ cup Triple Sec
¼ cup fresh lime juice
½ cup sugar
Kosher salt, to rim glasses

Strawberry Margaritas: Clean, stem, and freeze whole strawberries, or use 3 cups frozen in place of watermelon. Rim glasses with a mixture of salt and sugar, and garnish each with a whole strawberry.

1) Cut up flesh of watermelon into rough chunks. Reserve some small wedges for garnish, if desired.

2) Lightly coat a jellyroll pan with nonstick spray, and spread watermelon chunks in a single layer on the pan. Freeze several hours or overnight.

3) In pitcher of your blender, add tequila, Triple Sec, lime juice, 3 cups frozen watermelon, and sugar, in that order. Pulse blender to begin to break down frozen fruit, then whip until blended.

4) Invert each margarita glass into a shallow bowl of water just to wet rim, then into a plate of kosher salt.

5) Pour margarita mixture into glasses, taking care not to disturb salt rim.

6) Garnish with small wedges of watermelon, if desired, by cutting a slit into side to perch wedge on rim of each glass. Also fun to serve with a few mini chocolate chips for seed effect.

Bread, Breakfast & Brunch

Southern Buttermilk Biscuits

Prep time: 10 min **Cook time:** 12 min **Yield:** 6–12 biscuits

2 cups cold soft, winter wheat, self-rising southern flour (like White Lily brand)

¼ cup very cold butter, shortening, or lard, cut into cubes

¾ cup cold real buttermilk

1) Preheat oven to 500°. Coat a 10-inch cast-iron skillet or a baking pan with additional shortening or oil, and place in oven for 5 minutes.

2) Put flour into a bowl. Toss cold butter cubes in flour. Using a pastry cutter or 2 knives, cut butter into flour until it is crumbly. Add buttermilk, and use a fork to mix lightly. Dough will be very shaggy.

3) Put a bit of additional flour on countertop, and scoop dough out. Sprinkle a small amount of flour over top, and gently push together to form a rectangle. Do not over-handle dough.

4) Fold short sides in toward middle; turn dough, gently press down into a rectangle again, and repeat. Repeat this folding once more, and pat into desired thickness, about an inch thick. This folding creates flaky layers.

5) Using a biscuit cutter or rim of a small juice glass, cut out into rounds, taking care not to twist cutter. Gently gather scraps for last biscuits.

6) Carefully transfer to heated skillet or baking pan, and bake 10–12 minutes, or until golden brown on top and cooked through.

Secrets to Making Perfect Buttermilk Biscuits

1) **Preheat skillet.** Just as you do with southern cornbread, coat a cast-iron skillet with shortening or butter, or spray a rimmed baking sheet or cake pan with nonstick cooking spray. Preheat it in oven for about 5 minutes.

2) **Use very cold, self-rising flour.** And for best results, use a soft, winter wheat flour—like White Lily brand—it does make a difference! Place flour in a bowl in freezer the night before you plan to make biscuits. Do not substitute all-purpose flour.

3) **Use very cold fat from refrigerator.** It can be lard, vegetable shortening, or butter, but my preference is butter. Cut very cold butter into cubes. Cut into flour using 2 knives or a pastry cutter until crumbly. Avoid using your hands.

4) **Use buttermilk.** Use real buttermilk, not a milk and vinegar substitute. If you don't use buttermilk regularly, it will keep a while, so just keep practicing on your biscuits, or store in freezer.

5) **Cold dough**. A successful fluffy and light biscuit comes from keeping dough cold, and not handling it too much. Heat from your hands melts butter, so mix and shape biscuits in about 5 minutes. You do not want the dough to get warm!

6) **Folding.** After quickly kneading, push dough into a rectangle, and fold short sides in toward middle, one on top of the other. Turn dough, shape into a rectangle again, and repeat. Fold once more for a total of 3 times, and pat into desired thickness, usually about an inch or less. If biscuits are too thick, they will rise quickly and lean over. Folding creates flaky layers in the biscuits.

7) **No twisting!** Use a cutter 2–3 inches in size, cut them very close together, and take care not to twist the biscuit cutter, whether it be a cutter or a juice glass, but only push down and lift up on the cutter. Twisting will cause the fibers in edges of biscuit to close and result in a flatter and more dense biscuit.

8) **Spacing.** I like to bake my buttermilk biscuits in a skillet, which produces a crunchy crust on bottom and soft edges. You may also bake them on a half sheet, rimmed baking pan, or in a small greased cake pan. For biscuits with crunchy sides, space about an inch apart. For soft-sided biscuits, place close together.

9) **High temperature.** Bake biscuits in a preheated 500° oven for 10–12 minutes, or until golden brown and cooked through.

Prep time: 10 min | Cook time: 20 min | Servings: 4–6

Homemade Southern Sausage Gravy

Delicious milk-based sausage gravy, sometimes called sawmill gravy, is a southern favorite. Serve this delectable goodness over some hot homemade buttermilk biscuits for a little piece of heaven.

1 (1-pound) roll bulk pork breakfast sausage

1 stick butter, or ½ cup bacon fat or vegetable oil

¼ cup all-purpose flour

3–4 cups milk, as needed

½ teaspoon kosher salt

¼ teaspoon freshly ground black pepper

1) Brown sausage in a large skillet, breaking up and crumbling meat as it cooks. Stir in butter or bacon fat until melted.

2) Sprinkle flour on top of meat, and bring pan up to a medium-high heat. Cook, stirring often, for 5 minutes.

3) Slowly begin whisking in 2 cups milk until fully incorporated and mixture begins to bubble. Continue whisking in additional milk, a little at a time, until gravy reaches desired consistency.

4) Add salt and pepper to taste; mix well. Serve over hot, split biscuits.

Prep time:
10 min

Cook time:
25 min

Yield:
About 9
biscuits

Ham and Cheese Biscuits

2 cups self-rising flour

¾ cup chopped smoked honey ham

½ cup shredded Cheddar or Monterey Jack cheese

⅓ cup melted cooled butter or cooking oil

Up to ⅔ cup milk (enough to moisten dough)

To Freeze: Wrap cooled biscuits or Breakfast Sandwiches individually in foil, and store in freezer in a zippered freezer bag. To reheat, preheat oven to 400°, place wrapped frozen biscuits on a baking sheet, and bake 25–30 minutes, or until warmed through, removing foil last 3–4 minutes.

1) Preheat oven to 350°. Combine flour, ham, and cheese. Make well in center, and pour in butter or oil and most of milk, using a fork to combine. Add remaining milk as needed.

2) Turn dough out onto a floured surface, and sprinkle a little flour on top, kneading dough until smooth and no longer sticky.

3) Pat dough about ½ inch thick; cut out close together with a 2-inch biscuit cutter, gathering scraps to make last few biscuits.

4) Place on parchment-covered cookie sheet, spaced about ½ inch apart, and bake 20–25 minutes.

Breakfast Sandwiches: Prepare eggs by cracking each into lightly greased muffin tins, and gently breaking yolks. Bake in a preheated 350° oven for 10–15 minutes, depending on how well done you prefer yolks. Split each biscuit, and top with an egg.

Blackberry Preserves

2 pounds ripe blackberries (may substitute raspberries)

4 cups sugar

1 lemon, zested and juiced

Cook's Notes: Jelling time is an estimate; it may take longer to reach jelling point. Consult a professional canning resource for details on water bath canning. Pectin may be used, however, follow guidelines in package as brands vary. For a more jam-like texture, crush berries more thoroughly before cooking.

1) Sterilize half-pint jars and lids. (Number of half pints will depend on type and size of blackberries used.) Prepare a hot water bath.

2) Wash and sort though berries, picking off any stems or leaves, and removing any that are not firm and fresh.

3) Add half the berries to a large pot, with half the sugar. Very lightly crush with a potato masher; top with remaining berries and sugar; toss and lightly crush again. Add lemon zest and juice; stir, and let rest for 30 minutes.

4) Place over medium heat, and bring slowly to a boil, stirring until sugar has dissolved.

5) Increase heat, and cook quickly until berries reach jelling point at about 220°–221° on a thermometer, roughly 30–40 minutes.

6) Skim off any accumulated foam from top, and ladle into hot jars, leaving ¼-inch headspace. Seal jars with lids and rings, and process 15 minutes in boiling water.

Prep time:
10 min

Cook time:
20 min

Servings:
16–18

Sweet Potato Biscuits

These tender rolled and cut biscuits are infused with mashed sweet potatoes, and are great to serve with slices of country ham or other baked ham. They're especially good served with a little honey butter or a syrup infused butter, too!

BREAD

1 stick butter plus 1 teaspoon,
softened, divided

2 cups all-purpose flour

1 tablespoon baking powder

1 cup cooked and mashed sweet
potato

⅔ cup milk

2 tablespoons light brown sugar

1 teaspoon salt

¼ teaspoon each: (1 or more the
following) cinnamon, allspice,
ground cloves, ginger

1) Preheat oven to 425°. Butter 2 (8-inch) cake pans with 1 teaspoon butter; set aside.

2) Whisk together flour and baking powder.

3) Mix mashed sweet potato with remaining 1 stick butter and milk until blended. Add brown sugar, salt, and spices. Taste, and adjust seasonings for spices and sweetness.

4) Add in flour mixture a little at a time, working in until fully incorporated. Dough will be sticky.

5) Turn dough out onto a well-floured surface, and knead, folding dough in on itself and turning several times until smooth, sprinkling in additional flour as needed.

6) Pat dough to ½ inch thick, and use a cutter about 2 inches in size to cut out biscuits.

7) Arrange in cake pans, and bake about 20 minutes, or until light golden brown.

8) Serve hot with plenty of butter and sorghum, cane syrup, or maple syrup.

Cook's Notes: Leftover sweet potato casserole is perfect for this recipe. However, reduce sugar and omit spices as needed. These are especially good served with whipped syrup butter; blend 2–3 tablespoons syrup (sorghum, cane, or maple) with a stick of softened butter.

Prep time:
10 min

Cook time:
15 min

Yield:
About 24

Apple Fritters

GLAZE:

2 cups powdered sugar

½ teaspoon maple or vanilla extract

3 tablespoons milk, more or less

FRITTERS:

Vegetable oil, for frying

1½ cups self-rising flour

1 teaspoon baking powder

¼ cup brown sugar

½ teaspoon cinnamon

2 medium apples, peeled, cored, and chopped (about 2 cups)

1 large egg, beaten

1 tablespoon butter, melted

⅓ cup milk, more or less

GLAZE:

1) Combine powdered sugar, extract, and ½ tablespoon milk, adding more milk as needed, until you have a thick but still liquid glaze. If mixture is too thick, add additional milk 1 teaspoon at a time; set aside.

FRITTERS:

1) Preheat deep fryer to 375°, or heat 2 inches of oil in a deep skillet.

2) Whisk together flour, baking powder, brown sugar, and cinnamon in a medium-size bowl; add chopped apples, and toss. Add egg, melted butter, and enough milk to form a thick batter.

3) Use a small cookie scoop, or ⅛-cup measure, to carefully drop batter into hot oil, and cook until browned on both sides, turning over if needed. Drain on a rack over paper towels; let cool slightly, and dip each fritter in Glaze. May omit Glaze and dust with powdered sugar, or serve plain; serve immediately.

Real Southern Cornbread

I like to crumble a slice into a tall glass of sweet milk or buttermilk for a filling snack or quick lunch, or freeze any leftovers to use later for stuffing.

1 tablespoon plus ¼ cup melted fat (bacon drippings, vegetable oil, or shortening), divided

2 cups stone-ground, all-purpose white cornmeal

1 teaspoon kosher salt

½ teaspoon baking powder

½ teaspoon baking soda

2 cups buttermilk

1 large egg, beaten

1) Preheat oven to 450°. Rub 1 tablespoon fat on bottom and sides of a 10-inch cast-iron skillet, and place in oven to heat.

2) Whisk together cornmeal, salt, baking powder, and baking soda. Add buttermilk, egg, and remaining ¼ cup melted fat, and gently blend. Batter should be consistency of thick, cooked grits.

3) Use an oven mitt to remove hot skillet from oven. Carefully pour batter into skillet. Return to oven, and bake 20–25 minutes until golden brown.

4) Remove from oven, and let rest a few minutes, then either slice out of skillet or very carefully turn out onto a plate, and serve immediately. Cornbread is best served fresh and hot.

BREAD

Hushpuppies

Did you know that these simple fried balls of cornmeal and flour were actually born out of leftover fish fry coating? We tend to do them a little more on purpose these days and there are many add-ins to make them a stand-out.

1½ cups cornmeal

¾ cup self-rising flour

2 teaspoons sugar

½ teaspoon baking soda

¼ cup finely minced onion

1 large egg

1 tablespoon melted bacon
   drippings or cooking oil

¼ teaspoon each: kosher salt,
   black pepper, Cajun seasoning
   or cayenne pepper, and garlic
   powder

Chopped jalapeño peppers, sweet
   peppers, pimento (optional)

1 cup buttermilk, or as needed

1) Preheat deep fryer to 355°. Mix cornmeal, flour, sugar, baking soda, onion, egg, and bacon drippings.

2) Add seasonings and any optional ingredients you desire. Stir in ½ cup buttermilk, adding more as needed for a loose batter, but still thick enough to drop.

3) Spoon out batter or use a small cookie scoop, and carefully release into hot oil, frying until hush puppy floats, and turns a deep golden brown. Use a fork to carefully turn over if needed.

Cook's Notes: The amount of buttermilk needed will depend on the grind of the cornmeal. You want a loose batter, but one that can be scooped and dropped. Also okay to substitute regular sweet milk; you'll need less. When frying fish, substitute a tablespoon of fry cooking oil for bacon drippings in batter. These are excellent when fried in the same oil used for frying fish.

Prep time: 10 min

Cook time: 25 min

Yield: 12 muffins

Southern Pecan Pie Muffins

Five simple ingredients—and tastes like pecan pie!

1 stick unsalted butter

1 cup packed light brown sugar

2 large eggs

½ cup all-purpose flour

1 cup chopped pecans

1) Preheat oven to 350°. Line a 12-cup muffin tin with paper liners, and spray with nonstick baking spray.

2) Cream butter until smooth; add sugar, and beat until blended. Add eggs, one at a time, and beat in. Add flour and pecans, and fold in gently until blended; do not beat.

3) Evenly distribute batter between muffin tins, and bake 20–25 minutes, or until a toothpick inserted into center comes out clean. Transfer to a cooling rack.

Prep time:
10 min

Cook time:
30 min

Yield:
About 30

French Market Beignet Doughnuts

⅓ cup boiling water

2 tablespoons vegetable shortening

1 envelope (2¼ teaspoons) active dry yeast

¼ cup warm water (110°)

4 cups all-purpose flour, divided

¼ cup sugar

½ teaspoon salt

½ cup evaporated milk

1 large egg, beaten

Powdered sugar, sifted

1) Pour boiling water over shortening, and stir until shortening is melted. In a separate bowl, dissolve yeast in warm water, and set aside.

2) Preheat deep fryer to 360°. In a large bowl, sift 2 cups flour with sugar and salt. Add melted shortening mixture, evaporated milk, egg, and yeast mixture. Add enough additional flour to form a shaggy dough.

3) Turn out onto a lightly floured surface and roll thin, ¼–⅛ inch thick. Using a pizza wheel or knife, cut dough into 2-inch squares.

4) Carefully drop into hot fryer, and brown on one side until golden; flip, and brown on other side. Remove, and drain on paper towels; sprinkle with sifted powdered sugar, and serve immediately.

Prep time:
2 hours with thaw time

Cook time:
40 min

Yield:
2 loaves

Sausage and Cheese Bread

1 pound hot breakfast sausage

1 cup chopped onion

1 cup chopped green bell pepper

2 loaves frozen bread dough, thawed

1 cup shredded pepper Jack, Cheddar, or your favorite cheese

1 large egg, beaten with 1 tablespoon water

Stuffed Pizza Bread: Make this pizza bread by adding your favorite pizza toppings. Microwave pepperoni a few seconds, then dab with a paper towel to remove excess fat, and let cool. Use cooked, well-drained and, cooled ground beef, bacon, grilled chicken, or ham. Add veggies—onion, mushrooms, bell peppers, or jalapeños are good, though I do suggest sautéing many of them first. Let cool before adding to the bread dough. You can also spread a thin layer of pizza sauce on the dough, though I prefer to save the sauce for dipping. Mozzarella with a little Parmesan, Romano, or Asiago are great cheese choices.

1) Brown sausage in a skillet; remove to a paper towel to drain; set aside. To pan drippings, add onion and bell pepper, and sauté until tender. Remove to a bowl, and combine with sausage. Let cool completely.

2) Preheat oven to 350°. Coat a large baking sheet with nonstick spray; set aside.

3) On a sheet of lightly floured wax paper, roll 1 loaf dough into a long rectangle, about ¼ inch thick. Add half the sausage mixture along length of bread in center, leaving a border. Top with half the cheese. Brush edges of dough with egg wash, fold bottom part of bread dough up over filling, fold sides in, applying more egg wash, and then fold the top half over, pressing seam gently together to seal. Transfer to prepared baking sheet by lifting paper and rolling dough off, seam side down, onto baking sheet. Repeat with second bread loaf.

4) Brush loaves all over with remaining egg wash, and poke several vent holes into the top of each. Bake 35–40 minutes, or until golden brown.

5) Transfer to a rack to let rest and cool 5–10 minutes or until set. Using a serrated knife, cut slices about 1½ inches wide. Arrange on platter, and serve immediately.

Preserved Figs

BREAKFAST

6 cups whole, ripe figs (should be firm and slightly green)

1 cup water

4 cups sugar

Pinch of salt

1 lemon, scrubbed and sliced (optional)

Cook's Note: Consult a professional canning resource for details on water bath canning.

1) Pinch stems from figs, if desired. Rinse well, and drain; set aside.

2) Bring water, sugar, salt, and lemon to a boil. Boil until sugar is completely dissolved. Add figs, stir, reduce heat to medium low, and simmer 45–60 minutes, or until figs begin to turn transparent, gently stirring occasionally.

3) Ladle figs into sterilized jars, packing fairly tightly, and spoon syrup to fill, leaving ¼-inch headspace; seal with lids and bands. Process 15 minutes in boiling water.

4) Remove, and let cool on a heavy bath towel without disturbing.

5) If you don't want to process this with a water bath, you may halve recipe and refrigerate or freeze after cooking. They will keep 4–6 weeks in refrigerator without canning, or may be frozen for up to 6 months.

Prep time: 10 min

Cook time: 15 min

Serves: 4–6

Southern Skillet Fried Apples

A classic southern side, slices of apples are fried in a mixture of bacon fat (or butter) and brown sugar, then tossed in a dusting of traditional apple pie spices.

½ **stick butter or** ¼ **cup bacon drippings, or combination**

¼ **cup light brown sugar, well packed**

3 large Granny Smith apples, cored, peeled, and cut into wedges

¼ **teaspoon cinnamon**

¼ **teaspoon allspice**

¼ **teaspoon ground ginger**

1) In a skillet over medium heat, melt butter or bacon drippings with brown sugar.

2) Stir in apples, and cook over medium heat until apples begin to release juices. Reduce heat to medium low, and simmer for about 15 minutes, or until apples are tender.

3) Sprinkle spices on top, and toss until well blended.

Cook's Note: Okay to substitute apple pie or pumpkin pie spice for individual spices, so if you have those in your pantry, by all means use them here.

Old-Fashioned Coffee Cake

This very simple but classic and tender Old-Fashioned Coffee Cake comes together quick and easy. Serve with piping hot cup coffee, a drizzle of cream, or especially good with a scoop of vanilla ice cream for an unexpected dessert.

STREUSEL TOPPING:

½ cup packed light brown sugar

1 teaspoon cinnamon

1 tablespoon all-purpose flour

½ cup chopped pecans

2 tablespoons melted butter

COFFEE CAKE:

2 tablespoons melted butter

½ cup sugar

½ cup milk

1 large egg

1 cup all-purpose flour

½ teaspoon kosher salt

2 teaspoons baking powder

STREUSEL TOPPING:

1) Whisk together brown sugar, cinnamon, flour, and pecans. Stir in melted butter until well mixed, and set aside.

COFFEE CAKE:

1) Preheat oven to 375°. Butter an 8x8-inch glass baking pan. Mix together melted butter with sugar; add milk and egg; blend. Sift in flour, salt, and baking powder; beat until smooth. Pour into prepared baking pan.

2) Sprinkle Streusel Topping evenly over top, and bake 25 minutes, or until set. Remove from oven, and set aside to cool slightly.

3) Cut into squares, or serve with a spoon.

Cinnamon Roll Coffee Cake: Add ½ teaspoon vanilla extract to batter, increase cinnamon in topping to ½ tablespoon. Bake as above; when done, drizzle glaze evenly over warm cake. Prepare glaze using 1 cup powdered sugar, ½ teaspoon vanilla, and about 2½ tablespoons milk, adding milk a teaspoon at a time until it reaches desired consistency.

BREAKFAST

Prep time:
10 min +
30 min soak

Cook time:
15 min

Servings:
2

Custardy French Toast

Thick slices of leftover bread, soaked in a rich egg mixture, and dusted with cinnamon sugar, then pan-fried for a crispy outer coating.

4 slices thickly sliced day-old French bread, Texas Toast, or sandwich bread

1 tablespoon plus 1 teaspoon sugar, divided

¼ teaspoon cinnamon

3 large eggs

¾ cup whole milk

¼ teaspoon kosher salt

1 teaspoon vanilla extract

2 tablespoons butter

Powdered sugar (optional)

1) Place bread slices in a baking dish. Combine 1 tablespoon sugar with cinnamon; set aside.

2) Beat together eggs, milk, salt, vanilla, and remaining 1 teaspoon sugar. Pour egg mixture over bread slices; allow to sit for a minute, turn over, then sprinkle both sides with cinnamon sugar. Cover, and refrigerate overnight. (If using immediately, allow to soak 20–30 minutes until most of egg mixture is absorbed, turning again, if necessary.)

3) Melt butter in a medium-hot skillet, and using a spatula to transfer, cook on both sides until nicely browned. Transfer to plates, top with additional butter, and a dusting of powdered sugar, if desired. Serve with syrup.

Cook's Notes: French toast is also a great way to use up leftover hamburger buns, hot dog buns, or sweet quick breads, like banana bread.

Oven method: Bake in 500° oven on a generously buttered and preheated baking sheet, for about 8 minutes per side, or until puffy and golden brown. This is a helpful method when making French toast for a crowd, such as for a holiday breakfast or brunch with family.

Homemade Buttermilk Pancakes

My personal recipe for more than 30 years, these make simply perfect homemade buttermilk pancakes that I know you'll love.

2 cups all-purpose flour

2 teaspoons baking powder

2 teaspoons baking soda

3 tablespoons sugar

1 teaspoon kosher salt

2 cups buttermilk, more or less, divided

2 tablespoons butter, melted and cooled, plus more for skillet

2 large eggs

1 teaspoon vanilla extract

1) Whisk together flour, baking powder, baking soda, sugar, and salt; set aside.

2) Combine 1 cup buttermilk with 2 tablespoons melted butter, and eggs. Add buttermilk mixture to flour mixture. Gently combine, adding vanilla extract and additional buttermilk as needed. Batter should be fairly thick and lumpy, but pourable; avoid overmixing.

3) Heat griddle or skillet over medium-high heat; add additional butter, as needed. Spoon ⅓ cup measure of batter onto pan, leaving at least ½ inch between each. When pancakes begin to bubble up and edges appear dry, turn over to brown other side. Repeat with remaining butter and batter. Serve immediately with additional butter, warmed syrup, a side of sausage, and fruit.

Variations: Add in 2 tablespoons sour cream or plain yogurt. For chocolate chip or blueberry, pour batter into pan, then scatter some mini chocolate chips or fresh or frozen blueberries into batter; allow to set as usual, then turn.

Cheesy Eggs & Ham Breakfast

HAM:

2 tablespoons butter

½ pound fully cooked, boneless ham, sliced ¼–½ inch thick

½ cup cola or water

½ tablespoon apple cider vinegar

1 teaspoon cornstarch, mixed with a splash of water

¼ cup packed light brown sugar

¼ teaspoon dry mustard

EGGS:

6 large eggs

Salt and black pepper to taste

2 tablespoons heavy cream or half-and-half

2 tablespoons butter

2 ounces Velveeta cheese, cubed

HAM:

1) Melt butter in a large skillet; add ham, and lightly brown on both sides; remove, and set aside. Add cola, cider vinegar, and cornstarch mixture to skillet; bring to a boil. Cook until reduced and thickened.

2) Stir in brown sugar and dry mustard until sugar dissolves. Return ham slices to skillet, turn to coat, cover, and keep warm, turning several times.

EGGS:

1) Whisk together eggs, salt, pepper, and cream in a medium bowl. Melt butter in a large skillet over low heat; add egg mixture. Gently whisk in skillet, moving constantly, until very wet curds begin to form, about 7 minutes. Continue cooking over low heat until eggs begin to firm up but are still wet. Add cheese, and using a spatula, continue moving eggs around until cooked through.

2) Transfer to a warmed platter or individual serving plates. Serve immediately with ham slices, creamy grits, and biscuits or toast.

Cook's Note: Increase recipe as needed. I generally use 2 eggs per person, plus 1 extra for pan.

Creamy Southern Garlic Cheese Grits

A favorite southern breakfast staple, grits are taken a step up with the addition of garlic and cheese, making them the perfect bed for Eggs on Fire (page 49), or Gulf Coast Shrimp (page 147).

4 cups water

2 tablespoons unsalted butter

6 small cloves garlic, finely minced

½ cup heavy cream

½ teaspoon kosher salt

1 cup uncooked quick grits

2 cups shredded Cheddar cheese

Salt and black pepper to taste

Hot sauce (optional)

1) Put water on to boil in a medium pot over medium-high heat. Melt butter in a small skillet. Add garlic, cooking just until tender. Remove, and set aside.

2) Just as water is about to boil, turn heat down to medium, and stir in cream. Add salt, and then slowly add grits, stirring constantly the entire time you are adding them in. When grits begin to bubble, turn heat down to a medium-low simmer, and continue cooking, stirring often, until mixture is thickened and creamy, about 5 minutes.

3) Add garlic and butter from skillet, and stir in cheese until melted. Taste and adjust seasoning. Pass hot sauce at table.

Tomato Cheese Grits: Roast or sauté 4 Roma tomatoes in olive oil. Pulse in a food processor. Add to water with cream, with a small pinch of sugar.

Andouille Cheese Grits: Sauté ½ pound diced andouille sausage in 1 tablespoon butter for 3 minutes; drain, and set aside. Stir in with cheese.

Prep time:
40 min

Cook time:
15 min

Servings:
4

Eggs on Fire

A bed of fiery tomato sauce, made from fresh tomatoes paired with chunky diced tomatoes and green chiles and enhanced with bacon, onion, and sweet bell peppers, and then placed in oven to set, topped with cheese, and served over cheese grits.

4 slices bacon

½ cup coarsely chopped Vidalia or other sweet onion

¼ cup coarsely chopped green bell pepper

2 tablespoons tomato paste

2 medium-size tomatoes, peeled and chopped

1 (10-ounce) can chunky diced tomatoes and green chiles

Creamy Southern Garlic Cheese Grits (page 48)

4 eggs

Kosher salt and black pepper to taste

Shredded cheese (optional)

Cook's Note: If you prefer this on the milder side, omit canned tomatoes and chiles, and substitute an additional fresh tomato.

1) Preheat oven to 325°. Cut up bacon into a cast-iron skillet, and cook until just about crisp. Remove and set aside, reserving bacon drippings. Add onion and bell pepper to skillet, and cook over medium heat until softened. Stir in tomato paste and cook, stirring constantly, for about 3 minutes. Add chopped fresh tomato and canned tomatoes. Bring to a boil, reduce heat to medium low, and simmer 30 minutes.

2) Make a batch of Creamy Southern Garlic Cheese Grits (page 48) while tomatoes are simmering, and hold them over low heat, stirring occasionally.

3) Using a spoon, make 4 wells in sauce, crack 1 egg into each well; season eggs with salt and pepper. Using pot holders, carefully transfer entire skillet into preheated oven. Bake 10–15 minutes, or until yolk is set as desired. Top with shredded cheese, if desired, and return to oven just until cheese is melted.

4) Serve over hot cheese grits, and with thick, crunchy, buttery toast.

Prep time: 10 min

Cook time: 45 min

Servings: About 6

Hearty Breakfast Casserole

A yummy breakfast casserole that can be put together at the last minute—hash browns, sausage or ham, onion, bacon, milk, eggs, salt and pepper—what more could you want to start the day?!

4–6 frozen hash brown patties

1 cup (6 ounces) cooked crumbled Jimmy Dean sausage, or 1 cup cooked, diced ham

2 slices bacon, cooked and chopped

1 tablespoon finely diced yellow onion

1 cup shredded Cheddar cheese

1½ cups milk

4 large eggs

½ teaspoon kosher salt

½ teaspoon black pepper

¼ teaspoon Cajun seasoning (optional)

1) Preheat oven to 350°. Remove hash brown patties from freezer, and begin to thaw at room temperature.

2) Coat a 9x9-inch baking dish with nonstick cooking spray. Set aside.

3) Layer baking dish starting with hash brown patties. On top of that, add shredded cheese, then sausage, onion, and bacon.

4) Beat together milk, eggs, salt, pepper, and Creole seasoning, if desired; slowly pour over entire dish.

5) Bake 45–60 minutes, or until a knife inserted into center comes out clean.

6) Allow to set about 5 minutes before slicing.

Cook's Note: Double the recipe for a 9x13-inch casserole.

Soups, Stews & Chilis

Prep time:
10 min

Cook time:
30 min

Servings:
About 4

Grandma's Homemade Potato Soup

An old-fashioned, simple, chunky potato soup like Grandma made, with russet potatoes, onion, butter, evaporated milk, a little flour, and seasoned with salt and pepper.

2 pounds russet potatoes, peeled, cut into 1½-inch chunks

½ cup chopped onion

3 tablespoons all-purpose flour

Kosher salt and black pepper to taste

½–1 stick salted butter

Water to cover

1 (12-ounce) can evaporated milk

Shredded cheese, for garnish (optional)

1) Toss potatoes and onion with flour, salt, and pepper; set aside for about 10 minutes.

2) Melt butter in a Dutch oven or soup pot. Add potato mixture; stir to coat. Add enough water to cover potatoes, and bring to a boil. Stir in milk, reduce to simmer, and cook, uncovered, stirring occasionally, 25–30 minutes, or until potatoes are tender.

3) Taste, adjust seasoning, and continue to simmer, uncovered, until the soup reaches desired consistency and thickness.

4) Garnish each serving with shredded cheese, if desired, and serve immediately.

Cook's Note: Use an immersion blender or potato masher to purée potatoes if a smoother texture is desired.

Cheesy Ham and Potato Soup: Add 2 cups cubed smoked ham with potatoes. Just before serving, stir in 1½ cups shredded Cheddar cheese, just until melted.

SOUPS

Prep time:
10 min

Cook time:
15 min

Yields:
1 quart

Homemade Cream of Mushroom Soup

Use any place where you would use condensed cream of mushroom soup. I like to make a batch and freeze some to have it handy on busy weeknights. So much tastier than the canned variety, you will make it often as a stand-alone soup. Delicious!

½ cup unsalted butter

½ cup finely minced onion

¼ cup finely minced celery

1 (6.5-ounce) can sliced mushrooms, drained (or equivalent fresh), finely minced

1 teaspoon kosher salt

¾ cup all-purpose flour

3 cups chicken broth

1 cup half-and-half

Cream of Chicken: Eliminate mushrooms, and substitute ½ cup finely minced, cooked, dark meat chicken.

Cream of Celery: Increase celery to ½ cup, and eliminate mushrooms.

1) Melt butter in a large skillet, and sauté onion and celery over medium heat until tender but not browned. Stir in chopped mushrooms and salt; cook and stir 2–3 minutes.

2) Stir in flour, a little at a time, until fully incorporated, about 4 minutes, stirring constantly. Increase heat to medium high, and slowly add broth, a little at a time, until fully incorporated. Reduce heat, and simmer 15 minutes. Slowly stir in half-and-half.

3) Use about 1¼ cups to replace a can of store-bought soup. Makes a little over a quart, or roughly enough to equal about 4 cans.

Cook's Note: This is also delicious as a soup; just add 2 cups water to 1¼ cups condensed soup.

SOUPS

Made-From-Scratch Tomato Soup

Tomato soup made from fresh garden tomatoes and sweet Vidalia onions. It's a light meal even on a hot summer day.

6 extra large tomatoes

1 tablespoon olive oil

1 cup chopped Vidalia or yellow onion

1 stalk celery, chopped

2 cloves garlic, minced

1 tablespoon tomato paste

1 (10-ounce) can diced tomatoes and green chiles, drained

2 cups chicken broth

2–3 tablespoons brown sugar

2 teaspoons kosher salt

½ teaspoon black pepper

2 tablespoons butter

Heavy cream, shredded cheese, and chopped fresh basil, to garnish

1) Remove skins from tomatoes, and chop, reserving any juices.

2) Heat olive oil in a stockpot; add onion and celery. Sauté until tender, about 5 minutes. Add garlic; cook another minute. Add tomato paste; stir and cook 5 minutes. Add chopped tomatoes with juices, diced tomatoes, chicken broth, brown sugar, salt, and pepper. Bring to a boil; reduce heat, and simmer at least 30 minutes.

3) Use an immersion blender, food processor, or blender to purée, if desired. Add butter, stirring until incorporated; taste and adjust seasonings, as needed. Garnish with cream, shredded cheese, and basil, as desired.

Cream of Tomato Soup Variation: Add ½ cup heavy cream to soup pot, heat through, garnish, and serve.

Cook's Note: Substitute 2 (28-ounce) cans whole tomatoes when fresh aren't at peak.

SOUPS

Long-Night-Out Yakamein Soup

Yak a Mein, New Orleans Old Sober Soup, is most often made from beef, always includes boiled eggs, and is offered with condiments of soy sauce, hot sauce, Worcestershire, and ketchup. It's popular along the French Quarter after a long night out.

2 tablespoons beef base

1 teaspoon seasoned salt

2 teaspoons Cajun seasoning

1 teaspoon onion powder

4 tablespoons vegetable oil

Kosher salt and black pepper to taste

1 (3- to 4-pound) stewing beef roast (chuck, chuck tender, round, rump)

1 pound spaghetti noodles

8 hard boiled eggs, peeled (may be halved lengthwise, or cut into chunks)

1 green onion, sliced

Worcestershire, soy sauce, hot sauce, and ketchup (optional)

1) Fill a stockpot halfway with water. Add beef base, seasoned salt, Cajun seasoning, onion powder, oil, salt and pepper to pot, and whisk to mix. Place roast in stockpot (water should cover the roast, plus about an inch). Bring to a boil; reduce heat, and simmer 2–3 hours, or until beef is tender, and begins to fall apart.

2) Remove beef from broth, and shred using forks; return shredded beef to broth. Taste, and adjust seasonings. Hold soup over low heat until needed.

3) Meanwhile, cook the spaghetti noodles according to package directions.

4) For each serving, place some noodles in bottom of a bowl. Use a slotted spoon to scoop out a serving of shredded beef, and add to noodles. Add a boiled egg; spoon about 1½ cups soup stock on top, and sprinkle with sliced green onion.

5) Add a few dashes Worcestershire, soy sauce, or hot sauce, if desired. Some folks also like to add a bit of ketchup to theirs.

Cook's Note: To slow cook, place roast and seasonings in slow cooker, cover and cook on LOW 8–10 hours, until meat is falling apart. Then prepare as above.

SOUPS

Prep time:
15 min

Cook time:
30 min

Servings:
About 6

Southern Vegetable Beef Soup

2 tablespoons cooking oil

1½ pounds chuck roast

Kosher salt and black pepper to taste

1 cup chopped onion

1 cup chopped celery

1 cup chopped carrots

1 garlic clove, chopped

1 pound beef bones

¼–½ teaspoon Cajun seasoning (optional)

4 cups water

4 cups beef broth or stock

2 teaspoons beef base or bouillon

1 (14.5-ounce) can diced tomatoes

1 cup peeled chopped potato

½ cup frozen corn

2 cups frozen mixed vegetables (green beans, lima beans, field peas)

1 tablespoon dried parsley

2 cups dried egg noodles

1) Heat oil over medium-high heat in a tall stockpot. Season roast all over with salt and pepper; sear in hot oil on all sides until nicely browned, about 10 minutes; remove and set aside.

2) Add vegetables to drippings, sautéing 5 minutes. Add garlic and bones; cook and stir another minute, then add Cajun seasoning, water, beef broth, beef base, and tomatoes; bring to a boil; reduce heat to simmer.

3) Return roast to pot; cover, and simmer 1½–2 hours, or until meat is tender. Remove roast; when cool, shred or chop, and return to pot.

4) Meanwhile add potato, corn, and mixed vegetables to pot. Add parsley, and cook through, 15–20 minutes longer.

5) Cook noodles separately, according to package directions. Spoon into individual serving bowls; ladle soup on top.

Prep time: 5 min

Cook time: 40 min

Servings: 4–6

Mary's Favorite Hamburger Soup

A cafeteria lunchroom favorite, this soup from days long gone by is my all-time favorite.

1 cup chopped or sliced carrots

1½ cups chopped onion

¼ cup chopped celery

1 tablespoon minced garlic

1 tablespoon vegetable oil

1¼ pounds ground beef

2 (14.5-ounce) cans diced or stewed tomatoes, with juice

1 teaspoon kosher salt

½ teaspoon cayenne pepper

½ teaspoon black pepper

1 teaspoon dried basil

1 teaspoon dried oregano

4 cups water

4 cups beef broth

4 teaspoons beef base or bouillon

½ tablespoon Worcestershire

Splash of Kitchen Bouquet (optional)

2–4 cups frozen, or canned and drained, mixed vegetables

Egg noodles, cooked, drained

Grated Parmesan cheese

1) In a large soup pot, sauté carrots, onion, celery, and garlic in oil over medium-high heat until soft. Add beef, and cook through; drain off any excess fat, if needed.

2) Add tomatoes, salt, both peppers, basil, and oregano; cook and stir over medium high, 5 minutes. Add water, broth, beef base, Worcestershire, and Kitchen Bouquet. Increase heat to high; bring to a boil. Reduce heat to medium low; simmer 30 minutes, stirring occasionally.

3) Add vegetables; bring back to a boil; reduce heat to simmer, and cook until veggies are cooked through.

4) To serve, spoon noodles into soup bowls, ladle soup over top of noodles, and sprinkle with Parmesan cheese. Serve with homemade bread, or crusty rolls.

SOUPS

Crab and Shrimp Gumbo

2 tablespoons plus ¾ cup vegetable oil, divided

1 pound sliced okra

¾ cup all-purpose flour

2 cups chopped onions

1 cup chopped green bell pepper

½ cup chopped celery

1 tablespoon minced garlic

2 quarts shrimp stock or water

1 (14.5-ounce) can diced tomatoes

¼ teaspoon dried thyme

2 bay leaves

1 teaspoon Worcestershire

1 teaspoon kosher salt

Couple dashes hot pepper sauce

1 pound frozen gumbo crabs, cleaned and split

4 large blue crabs, boiled, cleaned, and halved, and/or prepared crab claws (optional)

2 pounds medium shrimp, peeled and deveined

Old Bay Seasoning to taste

½ pound lump crabmeat, picked for shell

1) Heat 2 tablespoons oil in a large skillet over medium heat; add okra, cooking until roping ceases, about 30 minutes; set aside.

2) Meanwhile in a large heavy-bottomed stockpot, heat ¾ cup oil. Using a wooden spoon, stir in flour. Cook over medium to medium-high heat, stirring constantly, until mixture is a milk chocolate color. Add onions, bell pepper and celery to roux; cook and stir about 5 minutes, then add garlic; cook another minute.

3) Stir in heated stock a little at a time. Add tomatoes, thyme, bay leaves, Worcestershire, salt, hot sauce, and okra; stir. Add frozen gumbo crabs and their whole claws. Bring to a boil, reduce heat, and simmer 1–1½ hours, occasionally skimming off any foam on top. Do not boil. Remove gumbo crabs, and add in blue crabs or claws, if desired.

4) Toss shrimp with Old Bay Seasoning, and add to the gumbo pot; cook about 4 minutes. Very gently, stir lump crabmeat in, so as not to break up the crab too much; cook just until heated through. Taste, and adjust seasonings as needed.

5) Serve in bowls over hot, steamed rice, and garnish each serving with green onions, if desired. Pass hot sauce at the table.

SOUPS

Prep time: 20 min

Cook time: 2 hrs 30 min

Servings: About 8

Dad's Oyster Filé Gumbo

My father-in-law's gumbo is a favorite of my husband, so I patterned this recipe after his.

1 (4- to 6-pound) hen or whole fryer, cut up

Kosher salt, black pepper, and Cajun seasoning to taste

½ cup vegetable oil

6 tablespoons all-purpose flour

1½ cups chopped onions

½ cup chopped green bell pepper

¼ cup chopped celery

2 garlic cloves, minced

3 quarts water

2 small bay leaves

½ teaspoon dried thyme

1 pound andouille sausage, cut into ¼-inch slices

1 pint fresh oysters with liquor (optional)

¼ cup sliced green onions

2 tablespoons dried parsley

Couple dashes hot sauce

1) Season chicken with salt, pepper and Cajun seasoning; set aside. Heat oil in a large heavy stockpot, and brown chicken on all sides. Remove chicken; set aside.

2) Prepare roux by stirring in flour; stir over medium-high heat until golden, about 15 minutes. Add onion, bell pepper, celery, and garlic; cook and stir about 5 minutes.

3) Slowly stir in water. Add bay leaves and thyme, and return chicken to pot. Bring to a boil, reduce to very low boil for 1 hour.

4) Add sausage, and cook another 1–1½ hours, or until chicken is falling off the bone, and liquid has reduced.

5) Scoop bones from pot; discard. Add oysters, green onion, and parsley; bring to a boil, reduce heat, and simmer until oysters begin to curl around the edges, 3–4 minutes. Taste, and adjust seasonings.

6) Serve over hot, steamed rice with hot French bread, and filé offered at the table.

Cook's Notes: For a basic chicken and andouille gumbo, increase roux to 1 cup oil and 1 cup flour; eliminate oysters; filé powder is optional.

SOUPS

Prep time:
45 min

Cook time:
1 hour 30 min

Servings:
8–10

Green Gumbo—Gumbo Z'herbes

Collards, turnip, mustard, or dandelion are a few good choices for greens, as well as kale, spinach, watercress, arugula, sorrel, chicory, cabbage, carrot or beet tops, and flat leaf parsley.

5 bunches or more assorted fresh greens (see above)

2 cups chopped onions, divided

4 garlic cloves, chopped

½ cup bacon fat or cooking oil

¼ cup all-purpose flour

2 quarts reserved cooking liquid

½ cup chopped green bell pepper

¼ cup chopped celery

Ham hock or ham bone

2–3 pounds assorted diced meats, such as ham or sausage

1½ teaspoons kosher salt

¼ teaspoon black pepper

¼–½ teaspoon Cajun seasoning

1 teaspoon fresh thyme leaves

½ teaspoon dried marjoram

2 bay leaves

¼ teaspoon freshly grated nutmeg

Red pepper flakes, filé powder, and hot pepper sauce to taste (optional)

1) Wash greens thoroughly; strip leaves from stems; discard stems. Roughly chop greens; add to stockpot; cover with water. Add 1 cup onions and garlic; bring to a boil. Reduce heat; simmer 30 minutes.

2) Scoop greens out of cooking liquid (reserve 2 quarts liquid); set aside 2 cups drained greens. Purée remaining greens in a food processor, and set aside.

3) In large heavy-bottomed pot, heat bacon fat; stir in flour. Cook, stirring constantly, until the color of peanut butter. Add remaining 1 cup chopped onion, bell pepper, and celery, and cook until tender, about 5 minutes.

4) Slowly stir reserved 2 cups cooking liquid into the roux. Add puréed greens, plus reserved whole greens to pot, and stir in seasonings. Add ham bone.

5) Sauté diced meat in a separate skillet with a bit of cooking oil. Add meat and pan drippings to pot of greens. Bring to a boil, reduce heat, cover, and simmer about 1½ hours, stirring occasionally.

6) Taste and adjust seasonings as needed. Serve over hot rice, sprinkle with filé, if desired, and pass hot sauce at the table.

SOUPS

Prep time:
1 hour 30 min

Cook time:
40 min

Yield:
About 1 gallon

Homemade Chicken Stew

SOUPS

1 (3- to 4-pound) chicken, cut up

2 teaspoons kosher salt

½ onion, cut into quarters

1 carrot, cut into chunks

1 celery stalk, cut into chunks

4 slices bacon

1½ cups chopped onion

¼ cup chopped green bell pepper

⅓ cup all-purpose flour

2 pounds russet potatoes, cut into medium chunks (about 4 cups)

1 (28-ounce) can whole tomatoes, cut up, undrained

3–4 (15-ounce) cans vegetables your choice, drained

2 teaspoons sugar

½ teaspoon black pepper

1 (12-ounce) can evaporated milk, divided

½–1 stick butter, melted

½ teaspoon crushed dried thyme

1 teaspoon Cajun seasoning

1 tablespoon dried parsley

2 tablespoons cornstarch

1) Place chicken pieces in tall stockpot; cover with water; add salt, quartered onion, carrot, and celery. Bring to a boil, reduce heat, and cook until chicken is falling off bone. Remove chicken; strain, reserving all broth and discarding vegetables. Debone chicken when cooled; set aside.

2) In bottom of same stockpot, cook bacon with chopped onion and bell pepper until bacon is rendered, but not crisp. Stir in flour; cook 3 minutes, stirring constantly. Slowly stir in reserved stock. Bring mixture to a boil; add potatoes; return to a boil, and cook 5 minutes.

3) Add tomatoes, canned vegetables, sugar, and pepper. Bring back to a boil; reduce heat, and simmer, uncovered, 30 minutes. Set aside ¼ cup evaporated milk. Stir in remaining evaporated milk, cooked chicken, butter, thyme, Cajun seasoning, and parsley.

4) Make a slurry of reserved ¼ cup evaporated milk and cornstarch; add to stew. Bring to a near boil; reduce heat, and simmer 10 minutes. Taste, and adjust seasonings, if needed. Serve with cornbread or crackers.

Prep time:
10 min

Cook time:
15 min

Servings:
4–6

Creamy Oyster Stew

SOUPS

2 cups milk

1½ cups half-and-half or heavy cream

1 stick butter

4 tablespoons all-purpose flour

⅓ cup finely chopped onion

½ teaspoon Cajun seasoning

½ teaspoon garlic salt

1 pint oysters, reserving liquid

3 green onions, sliced

Tiger sauce and hot sauce, for garnish (optional)

Crushed saltines, for garnish

Sliced fresh green onion, for garnish

1) Heat milk and half-and-half in a medium saucepan over a low simmer. Slowly warm mixture; do not boil.

2) In a separate skillet, melt butter over medium to medium-high heat and stir in flour, 1 tablespoon at a time, until fully incorporated. Cook and stir 2 minutes. Add onion and cook until softened. Stir in Cajun seasoning and garlic salt. Reduce heat to just under medium.

3) Slowly add warmed milk blend to roux about 1 cup at a time, stirring constantly until all milk has been incorporated. Do not boil. Drain oysters, reserving liquid; set oysters aside, and stir in oyster liquor, bringing it up to a slow simmer. Add the green onion, and simmer for 10 minutes, stirring frequently.

4) Add oysters and slow simmer until the edges of oysters begin to curl. Plate in a nice soup bowl, and drizzle each serving with a bit of hot sauce—I like the combination of Tiger Sauce and Louisiana hot sauce.

5) Crumble a couple of saltines in the center of each bowl, and garnish with a sprinkle of fresh-sliced green onion. Also very good spooned over homemade mashed potatoes.

Prep time:
20 min

Cook time:
1 hour

Yield:
About 6 cups

No Bean Beef Chili

DRY SEASONING:

1 tablespoon each: ground cumin, dried oregano, and chili powder

½ teaspoon each: ground cinnamon and Cajun seasoning

1 tablespoon sugar

WET SEASONING:

2 tablespoons each: Kitchen Bouquet and Worcestershire

½ teaspoon hot sauce

1 (6-ounce) can tomato paste

CHILI:

2 tablespoons olive oil

1 medium yellow onion, diced

1 medium green bell pepper, diced

1 medium red bell pepper, diced

Up to ¼ cup chopped jalapeños

2 pounds ground chuck

3 garlic cloves, minced

2 cups beef stock or broth

2 bay leaves

Salt and black pepper to taste

Garnishes: sour cream, grated Cheddar cheese, sliced green onion

1) Combine Dry Seasonings; set aside. Combine Wet Seasonings; set aside.

2) Heat oil in a large heavy bottomed pot over medium-high heat. Add onion, bell peppers, and jalapeños; sauté until tender, about 5 minutes. Add ground beef, and cook about 10 minutes or until meat is no longer pink. Add garlic, and cook 1 minute. Drain off excess fat.

3) Add Dry Seasoning mixture to beef, and cook 5 minutes longer. Add Wet Seasoning mixture, and cook 4 minutes longer. Add stock and bay leaves, and bring to a boil. Reduce heat, and simmer, uncovered, 1 hour. Season with salt and pepper. Garnish as desired.

Homemade Beef Chili with Beans

CHILI SEASONING:

½ tablespoon ground cumin

½ tablespoon dried oregano

1 tablespoon chili powder

½ teaspoon Cajun seasoning (optional)

CHILI:

2 tablespoons olive oil

1½ cups chopped yellow onion

1 cup chopped green bell pepper

1 (7-ounce) can chopped green chiles

2 pounds ground chuck

3 garlic cloves, minced

2 tablespoons Worcestershire

1 tablespoon sugar

2 teaspoons hot sauce

1 (28-ounce) can whole tomatoes, undrained, chopped

1 (14.5-ounce) can diced tomatoes, undrained

2 cups beef stock or broth

2 bay leaves

3 (15-ounce) cans light kidney beans, drained, rinsed, divided

Salt and black pepper to taste

1) Mix Chili Seasoning; set aside.

2) Heat oil in a large heavy-bottomed soup pot over medium-high heat. Add onion, bell pepper, and green chiles; sauté until tender, about 5 minutes. Add ground chuck, and cook 10 minutes, or until meat is no longer pink. Add garlic, and cook another minute. Drain off excess fat.

3) Add Chili Seasoning, Worcestershire, sugar, hot sauce, tomatoes, beef stock, and bay leaves; bring to a boil. Reduce heat, and simmer, uncovered, 40 minutes, or until liquid is significantly reduced. Mash 1 can beans, and add to chili. Add remaining 2 cans beans; taste, season with salt and pepper, and continue cooking on a low simmer, 20 minutes longer. Garnish with grated cheese, sour cream, and/or sliced green onions.

Cook's Notes: Chili is, by nature, spicy, so always start with a lesser amount of seasonings, then taste and adjust. May also substitute a combination of 1 pound ground chuck and 1 pound raw sausage, such as Italian sausage or Mexican chorizo, if desired. May also use a leaner ground beef or ground turkey, but some of the flavor may be lost due to the fat loss.

SOUPS

Salads

Old-Fashioned Seven Layer Salad

Topped with a mayonnaise dressing, this salad is a classic for parties, potlucks, church suppers, and holidays.

DRESSING:

1½–2 cups real mayonnaise

1 packet dry ranch dressing mix

2 tablespoons sugar

4 tablespoons half-and-half or milk

SALAD:

1 large head iceberg lettuce, shredded

8 Roma tomatoes, cleaned, seeded, chopped

Kosher salt and black pepper to taste

8 hard-boiled eggs, peeled

1–1½ cups frozen green peas, lightly steamed

½–1 cup chopped celery

8 slices cooked bacon, chopped

1–1½ cups shredded Cheddar cheese

Sliced green onion or chopped fresh herbs, to garnish

1) For Dressing, combine mayonnaise, ranch dressing mix, sugar, and half-and-half; set aside.

2) In a glass bowl, layer half of shredded lettuce.

3) Lightly squeeze chopped tomatoes between paper towels to absorb excess liquid. Arrange tomatoes on top of lettuce layer, first around outside edges, then working toward the middle. Sprinkle lightly with salt and pepper.

4) Slice enough boiled eggs to line completely around outside of dish; then chop remaining eggs, and cover tomatoes.

5) Top with peas, then celery. Sprinkle lightly with additional salt and pepper. Add remaining shredded lettuce; top with chopped bacon and shredded cheese.

6) Dollop Dressing on top, then spread evenly to edges to seal. Refrigerate up to 24 hours.

7) Before serving, top with sliced green onion. Serve as is for a pretty layered effect, or toss entire salad before serving.

SALADS

Cornbread Salad

DRESSING:

1 cup mayonnaise

1 cup sour cream

1 envelope ranch dressing mix

¼ teaspoon Cajun seasoning

2 teaspoons sweet pickle juice

SALAD:

2 (6- to 8-ounce) packages cornbread mix, or half a pan prepared

2 (14.5-ounce) cans black-eyed peas, rinsed and drained

2 (12-ounce) cans whole-kernel corn, drained

1 cup chopped purple onion

1 cup chopped green bell pepper

½ cup chopped sweet pickles

¼ cup chopped pickled jalapeños

1 cup chopped turkey, chicken, or ham (optional)

2 medium tomatoes, chopped

2 cups shredded Cheddar cheese

10 slices bacon, cooked crisp and crumbled

1) Mix Dressing ingredients; set aside.

2) Prepare cornbread according to package instructions; let cool completely; crumble into large bowl.

3) Layer remaining ingredients in order given, except bacon. Top with Dressing, cover; refrigerate overnight, or up to 24 hours.

4) Just before serving, top with bacon.

Optional Add-Ins: Shredded romaine lettuce, chopped boiled egg, drained English peas, drained Mexicorn, sliced green onion, red, yellow, or orange bell pepper, chopped, drained pimentos, black olives, drained white, kidney, or black beans, sliced summer squash, chopped celery, chopped nuts.

SALADS

Prep time:
10 min

Cook time:
none

Yield:
1½ cups

Wedge Salad with Comeback Dressing

COMEBACK DRESSING:

⅛ cup light olive oil or vegetable oil

¼ cup chili sauce

¼ cup ketchup

1 tablespoon Worcestershire

1 teaspoon Creole or other spicy mustard

1 cup mayonnaise

1 hard-boiled egg, chopped

2 tablespoons chopped sweet pickle or pickle relish

¼ teaspoon black pepper

Couple dashes hot sauce

¼ teaspoon Cajun seasoning, or to taste

½ tablespoon minced onion

¼ teaspoon garlic powder

SALAD:

1 head iceberg lettuce, rinsed, and cut into 8 wedges

Purple onion, sliced thin

Grape tomatoes, sliced

Chopped pimentos

Crumbled, cooked bacon

1) Combine Comeback Dressing ingredients until blended. May also process in a food processor or blender for a smoother consistency. Thin with a bit of milk, if desired. Store in refrigerator overnight before using.

2) To serve, drizzle each wedge with Comeback Dressing, and garnish with thin slices of purple onion, sliced grape tomatoes, chopped pimentos, and crumbled, cooked bacon.

Cook's Note: Omit the chopped eggs to use Comeback Dressing as a sandwich spread, or as a dipping sauce for crackers, veggies—everything!

Fire 'n Ice Summer Salad

One of my favorite southern salads for summer, this spicy, sweet Fire 'n Ice Salad gets its name from the contrast between the purple onion, green bell pepper, horseradish, and jalapeños, and the cool crunchy cucumber and sweet tomatoes.

DRESSING:

¼ cup apple cider vinegar

¼ cup red wine vinegar

¼ cup sugar

1 teaspoon salt

1 teaspoon horseradish

1 teaspoon celery seeds

1 teaspoon mustard seeds

SALAD:

1 medium green bell pepper, cut into thin strips

1 small purple onion, cut in half and sliced thin

1 jalapeño, chopped fine

3 large tomatoes, cut into chunks

2 medium cucumbers, peeled and sliced thin

1) Combine all Dressing ingredients in a small saucepan. Bring to a boil, and boil 1 minute. Set aside.

2) For Salad, combine bell pepper, purple onion, jalapeño, and tomatoes in a large glass bowl. Pour hot vinegar mixture over vegetables, and set aside to cool.

3) When cool, add cucumbers; stir, cover with plastic wrap, and refrigerate several hours. Use a slotted spoon for serving to drain excess liquid.

SALADS

Prep time:
5 min

Inactive time:
2 hours

Yield:
About 1½ cups

Buttermilk Ranch Dressing

½ cup mayonnaise

½ cup buttermilk

½ cup apple cider vinegar

¼–½ cup milk

½ teaspoon sugar

⅛ teaspoon dry mustard

1 teaspoon dried parsley

1 teaspoon dried minced onion

⅛ teaspoon crushed dried rosemary

⅛ teaspoon dried basil

⅛ teaspoon dried oregano

⅛ teaspoon garlic powder

Kosher salt and black pepper to taste

1) Whisk together all ingredients.

2) Refrigerate until needed, at least 2 hours.

SALADS

Forever Slaw Vinegar Coleslaw

A basic coleslaw, dressed with a sweetened vinaigrette, called Forever Slaw because of its long refrigerated shelf life, and a perfect barbecue side, as well as a topper for pulled pork.

SALAD:

1 (1-pound) bag tri-color coleslaw mix

1 cup chopped Vidalia or other sweet onion

½ cup chopped green bell pepper

DRESSING:

¾ cup white vinegar

½ cup vegetable oil

½ cup sugar

1 teaspoon kosher salt

1 teaspoon celery seeds

1 teaspoon dry mustard

Black pepper to taste

1) Combine coleslaw mix, onion, and bell pepper in a large, lidded bowl.

2) Combine Dressing ingredients in a medium saucepot, and bring to a boil. Pour over Salad ⅓ at a time, stirring in between. Cover, and refrigerate 24 hours.

3) Toss again, and let come to room temperature before serving.

Cook's Notes: May substitute a large head of cabbage, shredded. White vinegar is traditional for this, but you may use apple cider vinegar. It will give the slaw a slight yellow color.

Basic Creamy Coleslaw

A great cabbage coleslaw with a creamy vinegar and mayonnaise base, the perfect accompaniment for fried chicken or alongside barbecue.

DRESSING:

1 cup mayonnaise

3 tablespoons sugar

1 tablespoon apple cider vinegar

Large pinch of kosher salt

¼ teaspoon black pepper

2 heaping teaspoons prepared horseradish

1 teaspoon celery seeds

¼–½ cup bread and butter pickle juice

SLAW:

½ large head green cabbage

½ cup grated carrot

¼ onion, grated

½ (16-ounce) jar bread and butter pickles, chopped

1) In a large mixing bowl, whisk together mayonnaise and sugar until well blended. Whisk in remaining Dressing ingredients; set aside.

2) For Slaw, remove and discard outer leaves of cabbage, cut in half, and remove core. Coarsely chop or shred half, and place on top of the Dressing. (Bag and refrigerate remaining half of cabbage for another use.) Add carrot, onion, and chopped pickles. Toss until well combined, and cabbage is coated.

3) Refrigerate 1 hour or longer, tossing occasionally.

SALADS

Traditional Southern-Style Potato Salad

A simple traditional southern potato salad.

7 medium-size russet potatoes

3 hard-boiled eggs, chopped

½ cup minced onion

1 large celery stalk, chopped

1 teaspoon kosher salt

¼ teaspoon black pepper

1 cup real mayonnaise

1 teaspoon yellow mustard

**1 tablespoon chopped sweet
  pickle or pickle relish**

Paprika to garnish (optional)

1) Rinse and scrub potatoes, and place whole in a large pot of salted water; boil until tender but still firm, 15–20 minutes. (Test with a sharp knife.)

2) Remove potatoes; when cool enough to handle, but still warm, peel and cut into chunks or cubes, and place in a large serving bowl.

3) Add eggs, onion, celery, salt, and pepper, and toss.

4) In a separate small bowl, combine mayonnaise, mustard, and sweet pickle; spoon over potatoes, and toss again until potatoes are coated. Taste and adjust seasonings, as needed. Sprinkle top lightly with paprika, if desired.

Creamy Gumbo Potato Salad

Gumbo potato salad generally has no eggs or pickles in it, and is mostly mashed. It's perfect with gumbo, whether you scoop it right into the gumbo bowl, or serve it on the side.

2½ pounds Yukon gold, red, or russet potatoes

½ cup finely minced onion

1 large stalk celery, chopped

1 green onion, sliced

½ tablespoon dried parsley

¾–1 cup mayonnaise

1 tablespoon spicy Creole-style mustard

1 teaspoon kosher salt

¼ teaspoon black pepper

Paprika to garnish (optional)

1) Peel potatoes, and dice. Boil until tender and crumbly, about 20 minutes. Drain, and set aside. When cool, place into serving bowl, and partially mash, leaving some chunks.

2) Add onion, celery, green onion, and parsley to potatoes; toss.

3) In a separate small bowl, mix ¾ cup mayonnaise, mustard, salt, and pepper; spoon over potatoes. Toss again until potatoes are coated, adding additional mayonnaise for desired consistency, if needed. Sprinkle top lightly with paprika, if desired. Refrigerate any leftovers.

SALADS

Marinated Fresh Corn Salad

Super when served as a salsa with chips. Toss some in with your favorite pasta salad, too!

6 ears white, yellow, or bi-color corn, stripped of husks

¼ cup apple cider vinegar

¼ cup extra virgin olive oil

½ cup sugar, or sugar substitute

1 teaspoon kosher salt

½ teaspoon black pepper

1–2 teaspoons crushed red pepper flakes (optional)

1 cup chopped purple onion

1 cup chopped red bell pepper

2 large tomatoes, seeded and chopped, juices retained

¼ cup chopped fresh parsley

1 (15-ounce) can black beans, drained and rinsed (optional)

1) Cook fresh corn until crisp-tender, according to your favorite method. Drain, return corn to pot, and cover with cold water. Set aside until cool.

2) In a large bowl, whisk together vinegar, olive oil, sugar, salt, pepper and red pepper flakes until well blended.

3) Remove corn from cob, and add to dressing. Add onion, bell pepper, tomatoes with their juices, parsley, and black beans, if desired; toss. Refrigerate a minimum of 2 hours, stirring occasionally.

Cook's Notes: When local fresh corn is not available, substitute 2 cans whole-kernel or shoepeg corn, drained, or 1 (10-ounce) package frozen corn, thawed. May substitute commercially bottled Italian dressing, if desired.

SALADS

Prep time: 15 min

Cook time: none

Servings: 4–6

Tea Room Chutney Chicken Salad

A personal favorite, I patterned this chicken salad after a local tea room. Made with cooked, chopped chicken, purple onion, apples, grapes, and pecans, the secret addition of fruit chutney really makes it pop.

½ cup chopped celery

1 cup chopped purple onion

1 small Granny Smith apple, peeled and chopped

¼ cup chopped pecans

1 cup red seedless grapes, cut in half or quartered

2–3 tablespoons mayonnaise, plus more for bread

2 tablespoons homemade or commercial fruit chutney (mango, peach, apple, or mixed)

Kosher salt and black pepper to taste

3–4 cups shredded or chopped cooked chicken

Freshly baked, oversized croissants, or soft white or wheat bread

Curly lettuce and tomato (optional)

Minced pecans (optional)

1) Combine celery, onion, apple, pecans, grapes, 2–3 tablespoons mayonnaise, chutney, salt and pepper, and mix well.

2) Add chicken, and toss well.

3) Split croissants, and apply a thin layer of mayonnaise on both sides. Add a generous amount of chicken salad, and dress each sandwich with lettuce, and juicy, sliced tomato, if desired.

4) May also be served over a bed of lettuce. Sprinkle with chopped tomato and a tiny sprinkle of additional minced pecans.

SALADS

Deviled Ham Salad

Old school Deviled Ham Salad—as good as ever!

2½ cups smoked or boiled ham, (about ½ pound)

4 sweet gherkin pickles

¼ cup minced onion

⅛ cup minced celery

1 (3-ounce) jar chopped pimentos, drained

¼ cup real mayonnaise, more or less

2 teaspoons horseradish

2 teaspoons spicy mustard

1 tablespoon chopped fresh parsley

Dash of hot sauce

Salt and pepper to taste

¼ teaspoon Cajun seasoning (optional)

1) Use a grinder or pulse ham in a food processor until minced; add to a lidded storage bowl.

2) Grind or mince pickles, and add to ham. Add onion, celery, and pimentos, and mix together.

3) In a separate bowl, whisk together mayonnaise with remaining ingredients until well blended. Pour over ham mixture; mix well. Refrigerate several hours, or overnight.

4) To serve, spread on crustless white bread for finger sandwiches, and serve with a side of pickled okra and crispy kettle chips, or scoop onto a plate alongside celery and carrot sticks, and serve with pickle spears and crackers.

Cook's Notes: Grind or finely chop a few hard-boiled eggs to add in. For basic ham salad, use only ham, pickles, pimentos, and mayonnaise. For bologna salad, substitute ground bologna.

SALADS

Prep time: 10 min

Inactive time: 2 hours

Servings: 4–6

Shrimp Salad

A favorite seafood salad, made very simply. Serve on a bed of salad greens, as a sandwich, or stuffed into a tomato. Light and delicious!

1 pound seasoned, leftover cooked shrimp

3 hard-boiled eggs

1 stalk celery, chopped

1 whole green onion, sliced

3 tablespoons mayonnaise

Kosher salt and black pepper, or lemon pepper to taste

1) Roughly chop shrimp, and place in a medium-size bowl.

2) Peel and chop eggs; add to shrimp. Add celery, green onion, and mayonnaise; mix well. Add additional mayonnaise, if needed, for desired consistency.

3) Taste, season with salt and pepper, and mix well. Cover, and refrigerate to let flavors meld together.

4) Serve as a sandwich spread on fresh bread, or as a spread on saltines. Center a scoop on a bed of mixed baby greens surrounded by chunks of fresh garden tomato, or just stuff the insides of a nice fat tomato. Yummy!

Shrimp Seasoning Note: If you're using precooked or raw frozen shrimp, melt a tablespoon butter in a skillet and add thawed shrimp. Sauté until shrimp turn pink, or if already cooked, just to warm through. Sprinkle with some Cajun seasoning and a bit of Old Bay Seasoning to give it a bit of flavor punch.

SALADS

Prep time:
20 min

Inactive time:
2 hours

Servings:
About 8

Ham Pasta Salad

1 pound your favorite medium cut pasta (bowties, medium shells, elbow macaroni, rotini), cooked

Drizzle of olive oil

2 cups chopped ham

½ cup chopped celery

½ cup chopped Vidalia or other sweet onion

1 green onion, sliced

1 cup shredded or cubed Cheddar cheese

1 cup grape or cherry tomatoes, sliced

2 tablespoons pickle juice (optional)

1 cup mayonnaise

¼ cup milk

1 packet dry ranch dressing mix

Salt and pepper to taste

1) Cook pasta according to package directions; rinse and drain. Drizzle lightly with olive oil. To pasta, add ham, celery, Vidalia onion, green onion, cheese, and tomatoes; toss and set aside.

2) In a separate bowl, whisk together pickle juice, mayonnaise, milk, ranch dressing mix, salt, and pepper. Pour over pasta mixture, and toss to coat thoroughly; taste, and adjust seasonings. Refrigerate several hours or overnight.

3) Toss before serving, adding additional milk up to ¼ cup, if needed to moisten.

Optional Add-Ins: Chopped boiled eggs, sweet or sour chopped pickles, or pickle relish, chopped red, green, or yellow sweet bell peppers, jalapeño peppers, black or green olives, frozen peas, peeled and chopped cucumber.

SALADS

Prep time: 15 min

Cook time: none

Servings: 4–6

Seafood Pasta Salad

DRESSING:

1 cup mayonnaise

½ cup buttermilk, sour cream, or Greek yogurt

1 tablespoon lemon juice

½ teaspoon granulated sugar

1 teaspoon Creole mustard

¼ teaspoon each: garlic powder, onion powder, and dill weed

1 tablespoon chopped fresh parsley

SALAD:

2 cups dry medium pasta shells

1 pound small cooked shrimp

1 cup cooked, peeled crawfish tails

1 cup fresh crab, or 1 (8-ounce) package imitation crab

½ teaspoon Cajun seasoning

½ teaspoon Old Bay Seasoning

2 green onions, sliced

¼ cup chopped red bell pepper

¼ cup chopped celery

1 tablespoon chopped pickled jalapeño

Salt and black pepper to taste

1) In large serving bowl or lidded storage bowl, whisk together Dressing ingredients; set aside.

2) Prepare pasta; drain, and let cool. Place pasta on top of Dressing. Add seafood on top of pasta; sprinkle lightly with the Cajun seasoning and Old Bay. Add green onions, bell pepper, celery, and jalapeño.

3) Toss, taste, and adjust seasonings, adding salt and pepper only if needed. Serve immediately, or refrigerate until needed to further develop the flavors. If refrigerated, toss with a few splashes of milk to freshen before serving.

Cook's Note: If you are boiling your own shrimp, reserve leftover cooking water, and use it to boil pasta. It adds fantastic flavor.

SALADS

Prep time:
20 min

Inactive time:
8 hours

Servings:
About 8

Bacon Ranch Pasta Salad

This is my homemade version of a popular salad, made with small shell pasta, ranch seasoning mix, peas, carrots, and mayonnaise. It is a well-loved dish for a potluck, church supper, or any type of gathering.

6 slices bacon

1 medium carrot, grated

2 cups uncooked small shell pasta

Drizzle of olive oil

⅔ cup real mayonnaise

½ teaspoon onion powder

3 tablespoons (1 packet) dry ranch dressing mix

1–2 tablespoons milk

½ cup Le Sueur peas, or other young sweet peas, well drained

1) Cook bacon until crisp; drain on paper towels. When cool, chop and set aside.

2) In a microwave-safe bowl, lightly sprinkle grated carrot with water; cover, and cook on HIGH 2 minutes; set aside to cool. (May also sauté in a skillet, or boil in a saucepan.) When cool, wrap cooked carrots in several layers of paper towels, and squeeze out any residual liquid. Set aside.

3) Prepare pasta according to package directions; rinse and drain. Pat dry with paper towels. Transfer to a serving bowl, or storage container. Toss with olive oil to lightly coat pasta.

4) Stir in mayonnaise until well blended. Add chopped bacon, carrots, onion powder, and ranch dressing mix; stir. Add 1 tablespoon milk, and stir until creamy; add additional milk, if needed, for desired consistency. Stir in peas. Cover, and refrigerate for several hours or overnight before serving. Flavor improves as it sits.

SALADS

Ambrosia Fruit Salad

Ambrosia has become more of a fruit salad these days, but it started out very simply, once containing only oranges and coconut.

½–1 cup orange juice

2–3 tablespoons powdered sugar

2 sweet or sweet-tart apples, unpeeled, cored, and chopped

1 can mandarin oranges, drained

1 cup miniature marshmallows (optional)

1 cup chopped pecans

1 cup sweetened, shredded coconut

2 bananas

Maraschino cherries, for garnish

1) In a large glass mixing bowl, whisk together orange juice and powdered sugar.

2) Gently toss apples with orange juice mixture to coat. Add oranges, marshmallows, pecans, and coconut, and toss gently to mix.

3) Cover, and refrigerate until cold, gently stirring occasionally.

4) Just before serving, add sliced bananas, and give another gentle stir; taste. Stir in additional powdered sugar, if a sweeter taste is desired.

5) Using a slotted spoon to drain most of the juice, spoon into tall dessert glasses or cups, and top each with additional coconut, and 1 cherry.

True Southern Ambrosia: Peel and section 4 naval oranges, removing pith and membrane, so only flesh remains. Place a layer of oranges in storage bowl, sprinkle lightly with sugar, if needed. Grate fresh coconut (or frozen, thawed coconut) over top; repeat layers. (Do not use the shelf stable coconut.) Cover, and refrigerate overnight. Toss, and serve in small dessert bowls, spooning accumulated juices over each serving.

Prep time: 10 min   Inactive time: 1 hour   Servings: 12–16

Original Watergate Salad

Watergate salad is a well-loved fruit salad in the Deep South, and still makes an appearance at baby showers, bridal showers, parties, and even weddings.

- 1 (1-pound 4-ounce) can crushed pineapple, in juice, drained, juice reserved
- 2 (3.4-ounce) packages instant pistachio pudding mix
- 1 (16-ounce) tub nondairy topping (like Cool Whip), thawed
- 2 cups miniature marshmallows
- 1 cup chopped pecans or walnuts (optional)

1) Mix ½ the pineapple juice with pudding mix until well blended. Gently fold in Cool Whip, and carefully stir in pineapple, marshmallows, and pecans. Add additional juice only if needed—you want this to be moist, but not runny.

2) Cover, and refrigerate at least 1 hour, or preferably overnight. Scoop into individual clear goblets. Garnish with shredded sweet coconut, additional chopped nuts, and/or maraschino cherries, if desired.

Variations: Add 3–4 bananas, sliced, well-drained fruit cocktail, mandarin oranges, or maraschino cherries and/ or mix in cottage cheese with whipped topping.

SALADS

Million Dollar Sweet Pickle Relish

RELISH:

8 large cucumbers, peeled, seeded, and diced (about 2 quarts)

2 cups chopped onions

3 green bell peppers, chopped

3 red bell peppers, chopped

1 large can pimentos, drained and chopped (optional)

2 tablespoons kosher salt

SYRUP:

1 quart white or cider vinegar

4 cups sugar

2 teaspoons finely minced garlic

2 tablespoons mustard seeds

2 tablespoons celery seeds

½ teaspoon turmeric

¼ teaspoon red pepper flakes

RELISH:

1) In a large glass or plastic bowl, combine cucumbers, onions, green and red bell peppers, and pimentos; toss to mix well.

2) Add salt, and stir; cover, and refrigerate 6 hours or overnight, stirring occasionally. Drain well, but do not rinse.

SYRUP:

1) In a large pot, mix vinegar, sugar, garlic, mustard seeds, celery seeds, and turmeric. Bring to a boil, stirring regularly until sugar is dissolved.

2) Add in drained vegetables and red pepper flakes; return to a boil, reduce heat to medium, and simmer 30 minutes.

3) Use a slotted spoon to transfer relish into sterilized jars and top off with Syrup. Seal, refrigerate, or process for canning.

TO PROCESS FOR CANNING:

1) Sterilize jars and lids by placing in boiling water for 10 minutes. Remove.

2) Pack hot pickles and syrup into hot jars, leaving ¼-inch headspace. Add Ball Pickle Crisp® to each jar, if desired. Remove any air bubbles by pushing a spoon down sides of jar. Seal with lids and rings, and process in boiling water for 15 minutes.

SALADS

Vegetables & Side Dishes

Prep time: 10 min

Cook time: 60 min

Servings: 4–6

Green Tomato Casserole

One of the best side dishes you can serve.

4 or 5 green tomatoes, sliced ¼ inch thick

Couple pinches sugar (optional)

1 teaspoon kosher salt, divided

¼ teaspoon black pepper, divided

¼ teaspoon Cajun seasoning, divided

¼ teaspoon garlic powder, divided

¼ teaspoon lemon pepper

1 cup chopped Vidalia or other sweet onion, divided

2 cups shredded Cheddar cheese, divided

1 sleeve Ritz Crackers, crushed

1 stick butter, melted

1) Preheat oven to 400°. Butter a 9x13-inch casserole dish.

2) Slice 1 layer tomatoes into bottom of casserole dish—okay to overlap. Season with ½ the sugar, salt, pepper, Cajun seasoning, garlic powder, and lemon pepper. Top with ½ the onion, then ½ the cheese. Repeat with remaining tomatoes, seasonings, onion, and cheese.

3) Top with crushed crackers; drizzle melted butter on top. Cover, and bake 45 minutes.

4) Remove cover, and return to oven until top is nicely browned, about 15 minutes longer.

Prep time: 10 min

Cook time: 20 min

Servings: 4–6

Fried Green Tomatoes

There is a reason these have become so popular. Here 'tis!

3 medium-size green tomatoes

Kosher salt and black pepper to taste

¼ cup milk or buttermilk

1 large egg

1 cup self-rising flour

¼ cup cornmeal

¼ cup saltine cracker crumbs

¼ teaspoon Cajun seasoning

1) Slice tomatoes ¼–½ inch thick, drain on paper towels, and sprinkle both sides with salt and pepper. Let rest 5 minutes.

2) Beat together milk and egg in a small bowl; set aside.

3) Whisk together flour, cornmeal, cracker crumbs, and Cajun seasoning. Heat ½ inch oil in a skillet over medium-high heat.

4) Dip tomato slices in egg mixture, then into flour mixture; shake off excess, and place into skillet with hot oil. Cook 3–5 minutes per side, until lightly browned; drain on paper towels.

5) Serve immediately with a dab of mayonnaise, Comeback Dressing (page 70), or your favorite dipping sauce.

SIDE DISHES

Classic Southern Tomato Pie

Tomato pie is often served as a main dish when tomatoes are in season, but may also be served as a side along any main dish such as pork, beef, chicken, or seafood.

3 medium-size tomatoes, sliced ¼ inch thick (about 18 slices)

Kosher salt

2 slices bacon, cooked crisp, crumbled, divided (save drippings)

1 small Vidalia onion, quartered and sliced thin

3 cups shredded mozzarella, divided

1 (10-inch) deep-dish pie crust, partially baked, cooled

Pinch of sugar (optional)

Black pepper to taste

Garlic powder to taste

2 tablespoons chopped fresh basil

1 cup regular mayonnaise (do not substitute low-fat or fat-free)

½ teaspoon hot sauce

⅛ cup chopped fresh parsley

1) Preheat oven to 350°. Place tomatoes on paper towels. Salt, then cover with paper towels. Let rest 30 minutes.

2) Sauté onion in bacon drippings until soft, not brown.

3) Put ½ cup mozzarella into pie crust. Top with ½ tomatoes. Sprinkle lightly with sugar, if using, then season with pepper and garlic powder. Add ½ basil, top with ½ onions, and ½ bacon. Repeat layers.

4) Mix mayonnaise, hot sauce, parsley, and remaining 2 cups mozzarella; spread over top. Bake 40–45 minutes until light brown on top. Shield edges of pie crust with foil, if browning too quickly.

5) Cool pie before slicing. Serve warm or cold. Refrigerate leftovers.

Cook's Note: Interesting to use a combination of cheeses.

SIDE DISHES

Prep time:
10 min

Cook time:
1 hour 20 min

Yield:
Makes 1

Baked Vidalia Onion

In the oven or on the grill, these are so good!

PER ONION:

1 small Vidalia onion

1 garlic clove

2 teaspoons butter

2 teaspoons balsamic vinegar

Kosher salt and black pepper to taste

Cajun seasoning to taste

2 slices bacon

Cook's Note: Any variety of sweet onion will work, but don't substitute a regular yellow onion. It will be far too harsh, and you'll be disappointed.

1) Preheat oven or grill to 350°. Trim and peel onion, but leave root intact. Cut a very thin sliver off root end, if you need to level onion. Cut a 1-inch core out of top of onion; reserve scraps for another use. Peel garlic, and cut into slivers; stuff into onion.

2) Place onion onto a square of foil large enough to wrap onion entirely. (Double wrap, if cooking on grill.) Drizzle onion with balsamic vinegar, place butter into center of onion, and season lightly with salt, pepper, and Cajun seasoning. Wrap onion with 1 slice of bacon, then the other, securing with a toothpick, if needed. Seal foil tightly around onion.

3) Place onto a hot grill, or bake on a tray in preheated oven 1 hour.

4) Carefully open tops of packets, and return to oven or grill 20 more minutes, to crisp bacon. Serve as is in packets, 1 per person, or use a spatula to remove onion to a serving platter, pouring juices over top.

Prep time: 5 min

Cook time: 10 min

Servings: About 4

Maque Choux

Maque Choux is a very simple side dish of tomatoes and corn cooked in sautéed onion and bell pepper.

2 tablespoons unsalted butter

¼ cup chopped onion

¼ cup chopped green bell pepper

1 (15-ounce) can whole-kernel corn, drained

¼ teaspoon dried basil

Kosher salt and black pepper to taste

1 large tomato, peeled and chopped

2 teaspoons sugar (optional)

1) Melt butter in skillet, and sauté onion and bell pepper until softened, 5 minutes.

2) Add corn; cover, and cook on low 10 minutes. Stir in tomato and sugar; cover, and continue cooking another 5 minutes.

Okra, Corn, and Tomatoes Variation: Sauté 2 cups okra with veggies, add remaining ingredients, and proceed.

Cook's Notes: When fresh corn is in season, substitute 2 medium to large ears, cooked and removed from cob. May substitute 1 (10-ounce) package frozen corn and/or 1 (15-ounce) can diced tomatoes, drained. For variety, sauté 2 chopped slices bacon until tender, then sauté veggies in bacon drippings. Add butter at the end, if desired.

Prep time: 15 min

Cook time: 30 min

Servings: 4–6

Fresh Corn Casserole

A garden-fresh casserole featuring sweet summer corn and tomatoes, onion, sweet bell pepper, and herbs.

3 cups corn, scraped off cob (about 3 large ears)

5 slices bacon, divided

½ cup chopped Vidalia onion

¼ cup chopped green bell pepper

2 tablespoons butter

2 tablespoons all-purpose flour

½ cup sour cream

1 cup seeded, chopped tomato

1 tablespoon chopped fresh basil, plus extra, for garnish

1 tablespoon chopped fresh parsley, plus extra, for garnish

1 teaspoon chopped fresh thyme

Pinch of sugar

Kosher salt and black pepper to taste

1–2 tomatoes, sliced

1) Preheat oven to 350°. Butter a 9x9-inch baking pan; set aside.

2) Cook 2 slices bacon in skillet until crisp; remove to paper towel; set aside.

3) Chop remaining 3 slices bacon; cook in skillet. Add onion and bell pepper; cook until softened. Add butter and flour; cook and stir 3 minutes. Stir in corn, sour cream, chopped tomato, basil, parsley, thyme, sugar, salt and pepper. Transfer to baking pan.

4) Bake, uncovered, 15 minutes. Remove; top with tomato slices; bake 15 minutes longer, or until bubbly.

5) Crumble reserved bacon, and sprinkle on casserole with extra basil and parsley.

Cook's Note: May substitute 2 (15-ounce) cans whole-kernel corn, drained, or 3 cups frozen corn, thawed.

SIDE DISHES

Southern Creamed Corn

This is often called fried corn. Whatever name you use, I call it dee-licious!

2 tablespoons bacon drippings

½ cup heavy cream

½ cup half-and-half or milk

1 teaspoon cornstarch

6 ears corn, shucked, stripped, and scraped

1 teaspoon sugar

Kosher salt and black pepper to taste

2–3 tablespoons butter, or ¼ cup sour cream

Cook's Notes: May substitute 1 (32-ounce) bag frozen corn, thawed, or 3 (15-ounce) cans corn, drained, if desired. For more traditional creamed corn, remove about ½ the corn from skillet, pulverize in a blender, then return to skillet.

1) Melt bacon drippings in stainless or cast-iron skillet over medium-high heat.

2) Combine cream and half-and-half; whisk in cornstarch. Stir in corn and sugar. Pour into hot bacon drippings, and cook 15 minutes, or until reduced and thickened, stirring frequently. Stir in 2–3 tablespoons butter, and warm until melted.

Prep time: 10 min

Cook time: 20 min

Servings: About 4

Smothered Summer Squash

1 tablespoon bacon drippings

3 tablespoons salted butter, divided

1 cup chopped Vidalia or other sweet onion

½ cup chopped green bell pepper (optional)

2 pounds yellow summer squash or zucchini (4–6 medium), chopped, or halved and sliced

Pinch of sugar

Kosher salt, black pepper, and Cajun seasoning to taste

Chopped fresh herbs to taste (optional)

1) Melt bacon drippings with 2 tablespoons butter in large lidded pot or deep skillet. Add onion and bell pepper, and cook over medium heat 5 minutes, or until tender.

2) Add squash and sugar, and toss to coat; cover, and cook over low heat 20–25 minutes, or until tender, stirring several times.

3) Taste, season as needed with salt, pepper, and Cajun seasoning. Add remaining 1 tablespoon butter, and stir in fresh herbs, if desired.

4) Serve in small bowls, along with some of the simmering liquid.

Cook's Note: If using dried herbs, add in earlier.

Squash Creole

3 tablespoons butter

½ cup chopped Vidalia onion

½ cup chopped green bell pepper

2½ pounds summer squash, sliced or chopped

3 large tomatoes, peeled and chopped

1 teaspoon sugar

3 tablespoons all-purpose flour

1 teaspoon kosher salt

¼ teaspoon black pepper

Cajun seasoning to taste (optional)

1 cup shredded cheese, any type

1 tablespoon butter, melted

¼ cup bread crumbs

1) Preheat oven to 350°. Butter a 1½-quart baking dish; set aside.

2) Melt butter in a skillet; add onion and bell pepper, and sauté until tender, about 5 minutes.

3) Stir in squash, and cook until it begins to soften, 10–15 minutes. Add tomatoes, sugar, flour, salt, pepper, and Cajun seasoning; toss to blend. Taste and adjust seasonings as needed. Transfer to prepared baking dish, and sprinkle with shredded cheese of your choice.

4) Combine melted butter with bread crumbs, and distribute evenly on top. Bake, uncovered, 30 minutes, or until squash is tender. Let rest a few minutes before serving.

Cabbage Creole: Substitute 5 cups roughly chopped cabbage for squash.

SIDE DISHES

Prep time:
1 hour

Cook time:
2–3 hours

Servings:
8–10

Slow-Stewed Collard Greens

Southern seasoned collard greens are traditionally served with hoecakes or cornbread (page 37) on the side.

2 pounds smoked meat (ham hocks, smoked turkey legs, wings, or smoked neck bones)

2 large pinches kosher salt

½ teaspoon Cajun seasoning

1 cup chopped onion

3 cloves garlic, minced

Couple dashes hot sauce

2 large bunches collard greens

2 cups chicken broth, or more

1–2 tablespoons sugar

1 tablespoon bacon drippings or oil

2 tablespoons apple cider vinegar

2 tablespoons soy sauce

1 tablespoon butter

1 cup leftover ham pieces

1 teaspoon crushed red pepper flakes (optional)

1) Slash smoked meat lightly with a knife. Put in large stockpot, and cover with water, plus about an inch. Add salt, Cajun seasoning, onion, garlic, and hot sauce. Bring to a boil; reduce heat, and simmer 1 hour.

2) Clean, rinse, and chop collards.

3) To stockpot, add greens, broth, sugar, bacon drippings, vinegar, soy sauce, butter, and ham. Bring to a boil; reduce heat, cover, and cook 30–45 minutes for firm; 1½–2 hours for soft, stirring occasionally.

4) Add additional water or chicken broth, if needed. Taste, season with additional salt and pepper as needed; sprinkle with red pepper flakes, if desired.

5) Serve with vinegar pepper sauce at the table, if desired.

Southern Fried Cabbage

I like to add cider vinegar and dried pepper flakes to this traditional cabbage dish for a little extra flavor punch.

3 slices bacon

4 tablespoons butter, divided

1 cup chopped onion

10–12 cups chopped cabbage (1 large head)

1 teaspoon kosher salt

¼ teaspoon black pepper

¼ teaspoon Cajun seasoning (optional)

2 teaspoons apple cider vinegar (optional)

Dash of dried red pepper flakes (optional)

1) Chop bacon; cook in a large pot until fat is rendered. Add 2 tablespoons butter and onion, and sauté 4 minutes. Add a splash of water to deglaze any browned bits.

2) Add cabbage, salt, pepper, and Cajun seasoning to pot; stir. Simmer, covered, about 30 minutes, or until cabbage is soft, stirring several times.

3) Stir in remaining 2 tablespoons butter and cider vinegar. Taste, adjust salt and pepper, and sprinkle with red pepper flakes, if desired.

Variation: Add 1 (15-ounce) can diced tomatoes with green chiles.

SIDE DISHES

Smothered Okra and Tomatoes

3 slices bacon, chopped

1½ cups chopped Vidalia or other sweet onion

1 tablespoon minced garlic,

1 pound okra, fresh or frozen, sliced

3 cups fresh tomatoes, peeled, juices retained, or canned, undrained

1 (10-ounce) can mild diced tomatoes and green chiles, drained (optional)

1 teaspoon sugar

½ teaspoon kosher salt

¼ teaspoon black pepper

¼ teaspoon Cajun seasoning (optional)

1) Heat large skillet over medium-high heat; add bacon, and cook until crisp. Remove bacon, and set aside, leaving drippings in skillet.

2) Reduce heat to medium; add onion, cooking about 5 minutes, until soft. Add garlic and sliced okra to skillet (if frozen, no need to thaw), and stir-fry, turning occasionally, about 5 minutes.

3) Stir in fresh and canned tomatoes with juices, sugar, and seasonings. Bring to a boil, reduce to low, cover, and simmer 15–20 minutes, or until veggies are tender.

4) Stir in bacon. Serve immediately as a side dish, or as a main course over rice.

Iron Skillet Fried Okra

Sliced fresh okra, tossed in a seasoned blend of cornmeal and flour and shallow-fried in a cast-iron skillet.

1 pound small okra pods, cut into ½-inch slices

½ cup cooking oil, more or less, divided

¾ cup all-purpose cornmeal

¼ cup all-purpose flour

Kosher salt, black pepper and Cajun seasoning to taste

1) Rinse okra in a colander, and let drain. Heat ¼ cup oil in a cast-iron skillet over medium-high heat.

2) Combine cornmeal, flour, salt, pepper, and Cajun seasoning in a paper bag or medium-size bowl.

3) Toss okra in cornmeal mixture to coat evenly; transfer to skillet using large slotted spoon. Cook in batches, allowing to fry on one side until lightly browned, then begin to stir-fry, moving okra around the skillet, and scraping bottom of skillet to avoid burning.

4) Transfer to paper towels to drain, and sprinkle with sea salt or kosher salt. Prepare next batch, adding additional oil to skillet as needed between batches. Serve hot.

Cook's Notes: Choose small okra pods (3–4 inches in length), as they are the most tender. Substitute frozen okra if desired; simply place it in a colander, rinse well, and allow to drain.

Variation: Toss 2 green tomatoes, chopped, in with okra as you are coating it.

Brown Sugar Glazed Carrots

1 pound baby carrots, rinsed

1 teaspoon salt

Water to cover

½ stick butter

¼ cup packed light brown sugar

¼ teaspoon ground cinnamon

½ teaspoon kosher salt

¼ teaspoon black pepper to taste

1 teaspoon dried parsley

1) Boil carrots in salted water to cover until tender, about 8 minutes. Drain well; set aside.

2) To same pot, add butter, brown sugar, and cinnamon; cook over low heat until butter has melted and sugar has incorporated.

3) Add carrots, and toss until well glazed. Season with salt and pepper; taste, and adjust. Add parsley, and toss.

4) Transfer to serving bowl, and pour glaze over top.

Southern Fried Potatoes

Southern Fried Potatoes, also known as southern-style hash brown potatoes, are one of the most popular southern side dishes—tender inside, with crispy outer edges. Excellent served alongside eggs for breakfast . . . or anytime.

About ½ cup vegetable oil, bacon fat, butter, or any combination

2 pounds russet potatoes (about 4–5), peeled and chopped

½ cup finely chopped onion

Salt and pepper to taste

1) Add oil, bacon fat, or butter to a 10-inch skillet, and heat over medium high.

2) Add potatoes and onion; season to taste with salt and pepper, and toss to coat with oil. Cover, and steam 10 minutes.

3) Remove cover, turn with spatula in sections, and continue cooking over medium high, uncovered, turning and stirring occasionally, until potatoes are browned as desired.

Variations: Brown chopped andouille or smoked sausage and chopped green bell pepper in bacon fat, and add to potatoes before turning.

Loaded Twice-Baked Potato Casserole

2 pounds red-skinned potatoes (about 10 medium)

½ **tablespoon olive oil**

½ **teaspoon kosher salt**

1½ **cups shredded Cheddar cheese, divided**

4 slices bacon, cooked and crumbled, divided

2 green onions, sliced, reserve 1 teaspoon, for garnish

1 (5-ounce) can evaporated milk

1 cup sour cream

½ **stick butter, melted and cooled**

1 teaspoon chopped fresh parsley

½ **teaspoon garlic salt**

¼ **teaspoon black pepper**

1) Preheat oven to 400°. Scrub and puncture each potato; toss with olive oil and salt; place on a pan. Bake 45 minutes, or until tender. Let cool.

2) Slice potatoes in half lengthwise, then slice ¼ inch thick. Toss in large bowl with 1 cup cheese, ½ the bacon, and green onions.

3) Blend evaporated milk, sour cream, and melted butter. Add parsley, garlic salt, and pepper. Pour over potatoes, and gently toss or mash to desired texture.

4) Turn into buttered 8x8-inch baking dish; cover, and bake 40 minutes at 350°, or until heated through.

5) Top with remaining ½ cup Cheddar cheese, and bake, uncovered, until cheese is melted, about 5 minutes.

6) Garnish with remaining bacon and green onion. Serve immediately.

Cook's Note: Leftover baked potatoes are perfect for this recipe, so bake extra, or bake potatoes ahead to save time.

Slow-Stewed Southern Green Beans

If you grew up with slow-stewed green beans, the aroma of these cooking will bring you right back to your grandmother's kitchen.

2 pounds fresh green beans (not canned or frozen)

4½ cups water

5 ounces salt pork or fatback, rinsed and cubed, sliced or quartered

1 teaspoon black pepper

Cayenne pepper to taste

Salt to taste

1 tablespoon butter or bacon fat (optional)

1) Rinse, trim, and snap green beans in half or thirds.

2) Place into large saucepan with water, salt pork, and pepper; bring to a boil. Reduce to very low; cover, and barely simmer 1–1½ hours.

3) Taste, and adjust seasonings, adding cayenne and salt only as needed. Finish by stirring in butter or bacon fat, if desired.

Slow Cooker Method: Cook on LOW 4–6 hours.

Beans and Potatoes: Add whole (scrubbed) tiny new potatoes about halfway through, if desired, and continue cooking until tender.

SIDE DISHES

Field Peas and Snaps

1 pound shelled fresh, frozen, or dried field peas

10 cups water

4 ounces salt pork, bacon, or small ham hock

1 dried whole red chile pepper (optional)

2 tablespoons bacon drippings

2 cups chopped onion

1 large garlic clove, smashed

1 teaspoon kosher salt

¼ teaspoon black pepper

1 teaspoon sugar

1 teaspoon mixed dried herbs (such as Herbes de Provence) (optional)

1 pound fresh snap green beans, rinsed, trimmed, and snapped in half

1 tablespoon bacon drippings or butter (optional)

1) Rinse fresh or frozen field peas, and place with water into a large pot; cook about 30 minutes, or until tender.

2) If using dried peas, presoak according to package directions; drain and rinse. Cover with water; add salt pork and chile pepper, if using. Bring to a boil, reduce heat, and simmer, uncovered, 1 hour.

3) Heat bacon drippings in a skillet, and add onion. Cook about 4 minutes, or until tender, but not browned. Stir in garlic and seasonings. Transfer to pea pot.

4) Add green beans to pot; bring to a boil, reduce to medium, then simmer until tender, 25–30 minutes.

5) Add butter or bacon fat, and stir in; taste and adjust seasonings as needed.

SIDE DISHES

Prep time: 10 min

Cook time: 1 hour

Servings: 4–6

Purple Hull Peas with Okra

1 pound (about 4 cups) fresh shelled or frozen purple hull peas

4 ounces salt pork or bacon, chopped

1 cup chopped onion

2 garlic cloves, smashed

1½ teaspoons kosher salt

¼ teaspoon black pepper

¼ teaspoon Cajun seasoning (optional)

1 teaspoon sugar

4 cups water

8 small okra pods

1) Rinse fresh peas well, and sort through.

2) In a large skillet, sauté salt pork or bacon until fat is rendered. Add onion, and cook until softened; then add garlic, cook and stir a minute.

3) Add seasonings, sugar, peas, and water. Bring to a boil, skimming off any foam that forms. Reduce heat to low, and simmer 45–60 minutes, or longer, until peas are tender, adding okra pods the last 10 minutes of cooking time.

4) Serve with pickled onion and cornbread. We like to serve over a little rice here in the Deep South.

Calico Baked Bean Medley

A medley of mixed beans make up this classic baked bean dish. Great to bake and take.

BEANS:

1 pound roll breakfast sausage

8 slices bacon, divided

1 large Vidalia or other sweet onion, chopped (about 2 cups)

½ cup chopped green bell pepper

2 teaspoons minced garlic

1 (28-ounce) can pork and beans or baked beans, undrained

3 (15-ounce) cans varied beans (kidney, pinto, black, lima, butterbeans)

SAUCE:

½ cup barbecue sauce

1 cup chili sauce or ketchup

1 tablespoon yellow mustard

1 tablespoon apple cider vinegar

1 tablespoon molasses

1 teaspoon liquid smoke

Couple dashes Worcestershire

¼ cup packed brown sugar

½ teaspoon each: kosher salt, black pepper, Cajun seasoning

1) Preheat oven to 350°. Brown sausage in a large skillet. Drain on paper towels. Cook 3 slices bacon until limp but not crisp; drain on paper towels. Chop remaining bacon, and sauté until fat is rendered. Add onion and bell pepper; cook 4 minutes. Add garlic, and cook 1 minute. Add beans; return sausage to skillet.

2) Combine Sauce ingredients, and add to beans, cooking until warmed through.

3) Transfer to 9x13-inch baking dish, and add precooked bacon strips on top. Bake, uncovered, 30–45 minutes or until bubbly and warmed through.

New Year's Black-Eyed Peas

Black-eyed peas, cooked down with some bacon, jalapeño, a ham bone or ham hock, and a few seasonings, makes for a traditional southern meal.

¼ pound bacon, chopped

1 cup chopped onion

½ medium green bell pepper, chopped

½ cup chopped celery

2 cloves garlic, minced

Leftover diced ham and/or a ham bone or ham hocks

1 pound dried black-eyed peas, rinsed and picked through

2 quarts hot water, or chicken broth or stock

1–2 jalapeños, ribs and seeds removed, chopped (optional)

Couple pinches kosher salt

¼–½ teaspoon black pepper

¼ teaspoon Cajun seasoning (optional)

2 bay leaves

Additional water or chicken broth (optional)

1) In a tall stockpot, fry bacon until cooked but not crisp; add onion, bell pepper, and celery to the rendered bacon fat, and cook just until tender. Add garlic, and cook another minute or so. If you have leftover ham, add it also, and cook until browned.

2) Toss peas into pot, and lightly stir-fry.

3) Slowly stir in the hot water, then bring to a full boil.

4) If you're lucky enough to have a ham bone, stick it in there after you add water but before you add peas, reduce heat to medium, and allow the ham bone to cook by itself for about an hour to deepen the stock. Once that cooks (or if you don't happen to have a ham bone), go ahead and just add dried peas and then the jalapeño, salt, pepper, Cajun seasoning, and bay leaves. Then bring it all to a boil.

5) Reduce to medium simmer and partially cover, cooking for 1–1½ hours, or until peas are tender and creamy. Add additional water or chicken broth, only if necessary, to slightly thin out. Serve over hot steamed rice.

SIDE DISHES

Black-Eyed Pea Jambalaya

This is my Deep South version of the low country favorite, Hoppin' John.

6 slices bacon, chopped

1 cup chopped onion

½ cup chopped green bell pepper

¼ cup chopped celery

1 teaspoon minced garlic

1½ cups diced ham

**½ pound andouille or other
smoked sausage, sliced**

3 cups chicken broth or stock

2 cans black-eyed peas, undrained

2 cups uncooked, long-grain rice

**¼ cup chopped, sliced pickled
jalapeño**

¼ cup sliced green onions

2 pinches kosher salt

½ teaspoon black pepper

¼–½ teaspoon Cajun seasoning

1 bay leaf

Hot sauce, for table

1) In large skillet, sauté bacon until slightly browned. Add onion, bell pepper, and celery; sauté about 5 minutes until soft. Add garlic, and cook 1 minute.

2) Add ham and sausage, and cook another 3 minutes. Add broth and black-eyed peas; bring to a boil.

3) Stir in rice, jalapeño, and green onions. Season with salt, pepper, and Cajun seasoning. Add bay leaf, and return to a boil; cover, reduce heat, and simmer 30 minutes.

4) Remove from heat, and allow to sit, covered, another 10 minutes before serving. Discard bay leaf. Fluff with a fork. Pass hot sauce at the table.

Creamy Butter Beans

1 pound dried large lima beans

1 tablespoon bacon fat, butter, or vegetable oil

½ cup chopped onion

½ cup chopped celery

¼ cup chopped carrot

2 garlic cloves, chopped

1 teaspoon dried thyme

¼ teaspoon black pepper

2 cups chopped smoked ham

Meaty ham bone, 2–3 ham hocks, or smoked turkey wings

1 (32-ounce) carton chicken broth

4 cups water

2 bay leaves

½ stick butter (optional)

2 tablespoons dried parsley

Pinches of Cajun seasoning and kosher salt

1) Rinse and sort beans; place into stockpot with just enough water to cover them, plus about an inch. Bring to a boil, cover, and turn off the burner. Let soak, covered, 1 hour; drain, and set aside.

2) Meanwhile, in soup pot, heat bacon fat over medium heat; add onion, celery, carrot, and garlic, and sauté just until tender. Add thyme and pepper, and stir; add chopped ham and ham bone, ham hocks, or smoked turkey wings, chicken stock, 4 cups water, and bay leaves. Bring to a boil, reduce heat to medium, and simmer about 1 hour.

3) Add drained beans to soup pot. Stir in butter, parsley, and Cajun seasoning. Continue cooking on a low simmer an additional 60–90 minutes, or until beans are tender and sauce thickens. Add additional chicken broth or water only if needed. When beans are tender, taste, and adjust seasonings if needed; cover, and hold over very low heat.

4) Remove bay leaves, and serve. Also delicious over hot steamed rice with a side of cast-iron skillet cornbread.

SIDE DISHES

Cajun White Beans with Rice

1 pound package dried white beans (Great Northern or navy)

1 tablespoon cooking oil

1 pound andouille or other spicy smoked sausage, quartered and sliced into bite-size pieces

2 slices bacon, chopped

1 medium onion, chopped

½ green bell pepper, chopped

1 stalk celery, chopped

3 cloves garlic, minced

2 green onions, sliced

1 tablespoon dried parsley

1 teaspoon Cajun seasoning

Kosher salt and freshly cracked black pepper to taste

1) Rinse and sort through beans, and soak overnight. Drain, and return to pot.

2) Heat oil in skillet over medium-high heat. Add sausage, and cook until browned. Using a slotted spoon, add to beans.

3) To drippings in skillet, add bacon; cook until rendered. Remove bacon, and add to bean pot. Add onion, bell pepper, and celery to skillet. Cook until just browned and beginning to caramelize. Add garlic, and cook another minute. Transfer to stockpot. Deglaze skillet with a bit of water, and scrape up any browned bits. Add to pot.

4) Cover bean mixture with water, plus about an inch and a half, and bring to a boil. Reduce heat; simmer 1½ hours, stirring occasionally, or until beans are tender and thickened. Add additional water, if needed, to thin.

5) Stir in green onions, parsley, Cajun seasoning, salt and pepper, and simmer 5 minutes. Taste and adjust seasonings. Serve over hot rice with cornbread, and pass the hot sauce at the table.

SIDE DISHES

Prep time: 10 min

Cook time: 10 min

Servings: 4–6

Skillet Red Beans and Rice

A quick skillet version of red beans and rice, made with canned kidney beans, the trinity of vegetables, and cooked with instant rice—great for those busy workdays.

1 tablespoon butter or oil

½ pound andouille or other smoked sausage, chopped

1 slice bacon

1 cup chopped onion

½ cup chopped green or red bell pepper, or a combination

¼ cup chopped celery

1 tablespoon minced garlic

2 cups chicken stock or broth

½ teaspoon Italian seasoning

¼–½ teaspoon Cajun seasoning

¼ teaspoon black pepper

1 large bay leaf

2 (15.5-ounce) cans kidney beans, rinsed and drained, divided

2 cups instant rice

1) Have all ingredients ready. Heat oil in a large lidded skillet over medium-high heat. Add sausage and bacon, and cook until lightly browned, about 4 minutes.

2) Add onion, bell pepper, and celery; cook and stir until vegetables are tender, about 5 minutes.

3) Add garlic and cook, stirring constantly, another 2 minutes. Add broth, Italian seasoning, Cajun seasoning, pepper, and bay leaf. Bring to a boil.

4) Add beans and rice; stir together well, reduce heat to medium low, and cook, covered, 10–15 minutes, or until rice is tender. Fluff with a fork, taste, and adjust seasonings as needed; remove bay leaf, and serve immediately.

Cook's Notes: Taste first before adding salt. I recommend using a spicy andouille, Cajun-style sausage, or Alabama Conecuh, but if so, go light on the Cajun seasoning until tasting. You may also substitute any regular, mild smoked sausage, and adjust seasonings to taste. Great as a filling for burritos.

SIDE DISHES

Cajun Dirty Rice

Authentic dirty rice usually contains gizzards and livers, or some other form of giblets, but don't fret if you don't like them. Simply increase the beef or pork, and you still have a wonderful dish. Take it easy on the Cajun seasoning though—add a little, taste, and adjust!

3 slices bacon, chopped

1 cup chopped onion

½ cup chopped green bell pepper

¼ cup chopped celery

3 garlic cloves, chopped

2 tablespoons chopped jalapeños

1 pound mixed chicken livers and gizzards (or combination giblets), trimmed, rinsed, and ground or finely chopped

1 pound ground beef or pork

1½ teaspoons kosher salt

¼–½ teaspoon black pepper

1 teaspoon Cajun seasoning

4 cups cooked rice

¼ cup chopped green onions

1) Sauté bacon in cast-iron pot until cooked, but not crisp. Remove bacon, and set aside.

2) In bacon drippings, sauté onion, bell pepper, and celery, about 5 minutes. Add garlic and jalapeño; cook 1 minute. Add meats, and cook until lightly browned. Do not drain. Add salt, pepper, Cajun seasoning, and bacon; reduce heat to medium low, cover, and simmer 20 minutes, stirring occasionally.

3) Stir in rice and green onions; cover, and heat through, stirring occasionally. (May be kept covered on very low heat and steamed until ready to serve.) Offer hot sauce at table.

Creole Dirty Rice: Add 2 (10-ounce) cans diced tomatoes with green chiles, drained, 1 (15-ounce) can diced tomatoes, drained, and 1 (8-ounce) tomato sauce.

Homemade Yellow Rice

½ cup chopped onion

¼ cup chopped green bell pepper or jalapeño

⅛ cup chopped celery

2 teaspoons chopped garlic

1 tablespoon bacon drippings or butter

1 cup long-grain white rice

1 (2-ounce) jar chopped pimento, drained

2 cups chicken broth

½ teaspoon turmeric

½ teaspoon Cajun seasoning

2 tablespoons butter

1) Sauté onion, green pepper, celery, and garlic in bacon drippings until tender, about 5 minutes; add rice and pimento.

2) Whisk together broth, turmeric, and Cajun seasoning. Add butter, and bring to a boil. Reduce to low, stir, cover, and without lifting the lid, simmer 25 minutes, or until rice has absorbed all liquid.

Variation: Stir in ¼ cup chopped fresh broccoli, julienned fresh carrots, and/or whole-kernel corn with the rice.

SIDE DISHES

Bacon and Egg Fried Rice

2 tablespoons peanut oil

½ pound bacon

2 green onions, sliced

2 cloves garlic, minced

1 tablespoon low-sodium soy sauce

1 heaping teaspoon light brown sugar

1½–2 cups cooked rice

¼–½ tomato, seeded and chopped

½ cup frozen peas

2 large eggs, beaten

Salt and pepper to taste

1) Have everything ready to go. Heat peanut oil in heavy-bottomed skillet or wok. Add bacon, and cook until fat is rendered but bacon is still soft.

2) Add green onions and garlic, and stir-fry 1 minute. Blend together soy sauce and brown sugar. Add to skillet, and cook an additional 2 minutes, stirring constantly.

3) Add rice, tomato, and peas, and stir-fry 2–3 minutes.

4) Make a well in center of rice mixture, and pour in eggs. Cook slightly, then scramble eggs by moving around a bit, but still keeping in center of skillet.

5) Once eggs set, drag rice mixture into middle, and turn; repeat until egg is incorporated into rice mixture, and everything is warmed through. Season with salt and pepper.

Ham and Egg Pasta

½ teaspoon kosher salt

¼ teaspoon black pepper

1 tablespoon dried parsley

½ cup freshly grated Parmesan

½ pound angel hair pasta

Big pinch of kosher salt

1 tablespoon olive oil

½ cup chopped country ham,
   bacon, or andouille sausage

1 large garlic clove, minced

2 large egg yolks, beaten

1) Mix together salt, pepper, parsley, and Parmesan in a small bowl; set aside.

2) Cook pasta with salt until al dente, about a minute less than package directions; drain.

3) Heat oil over medium heat, and sauté ham until crisp. Remove, and set aside.

4) Sauté garlic in drippings; add pasta, and toss with Parmesan mixture. Remove pan from heat, add eggs, and continue tossing until everything is well blended. Serve immediately.

Cook's Note: Although the hot pasta cooks the egg yolk, a caution is extended to children, the elderly, and those with compromised immune systems who may need to avoid dishes using raw eggs.

Prep time:
10 min

Cook time:
25 min

Servings:
About 4

Macaroni and Tomatoes with Andouille

Macaroni and tomatoes is a depression-era dish that so many folks have handed down. In its purest form, it's simply lightly stewed tomatoes and macaroni, stirred in, maybe a little butter, and salt and pepper. I paired it up with spicy andouille for a little Deep South Cajun kick.

8 ounces elbow macaroni (about 1½ cups dry)

1 pound andouille or other spicy smoked sausage, sliced

½ tablespoon bacon drippings, butter, or cooking oil

1 cup chopped onion

2 (14.5-ounce) cans stewed tomatoes, undrained

1 small bay leaf

Kosher salt, black pepper, and/ or Cajun seasoning to taste (optional)

½ tablespoon butter

1) Boil macaroni to al dente according to package directions in well salted water. Drain; place into serving bowl; set aside.

2) Sauté sausage in bacon drippings over medium heat, about 4 minutes. Add onion; cook and stir another 3 minutes.

3) Add tomatoes with their juices, and bay leaf; bring to a boil; reduce heat to low. Simmer 20 minutes at a very low bubble, stirring occasionally, and using a spoon to break up tomatoes. Taste, and add salt, pepper, and Cajun seasoning, if needed.

4) Stir in butter, then pour mixture over macaroni. Let rest until ready to serve, then stir to combine. Discard bay leaf before serving.

Cook's Notes: The andouille may be omitted entirely for a more classic macaroni and tomatoes. If using fresh tomatoes, add 2 teaspoons sugar, ½ teaspoon dried Italian seasoning, and ⅛ teaspoon garlic powder.

SIDE DISHES

Prep time:
20 min

Bake time:
35 min

Servings:
About 12

Special Occasion Macaroni and Cheese

2 pounds medium-size elbow macaroni

1 pound sharp Cheddar cheese

1 pound Monterey Jack cheese

2–2½ cups whole milk

1 (2-pound) block original Velveeta, cut into chunks

4 large eggs

Kosher salt, black pepper, and Cajun seasoning to taste

2 sticks butter, sliced thin

Cook's Notes: This makes a big holiday crowd batch, but halves nicely. Avoid substituting preshredded cheeses, as they contain fillers and stablizers that affect results.

1) Preheat oven to 375°. Spray a large baking dish with nonstick cooking spray.

2) Boil macaroni; rinse, drain, and set aside. Shred Cheddar and Monterey Jack cheeses into a large bowl.

3) Pour 2 cups milk into large saucepan; warm over medium-low heat. Add Velveeta, Cheddar, and Monterey Jack, and heat until melted, stirring constantly. Add additional milk only if needed to thin. Remove from heat, and set aside.

4) Crack eggs into a separate bowl, and lightly whisk. Scoop out some cheese sauce, and slowly add to eggs to temper them, continuously whisking. Once well-tempered, add eggs to cheese sauce, and mix well.

5) Add ½ the macaroni to baking dish; season with salt, pepper, and Cajun seasoning. Cut thin pats of 1 stick butter on top of macaroni. Ladle ½ the cheese sauce over macaroni. Repeat layers of macaroni, seasoning, butter, and cheese sauce.

6) Bake, uncovered, 30–35 minutes, or until bubbly and browned.

Chicken

Prep time:
10 min

Cook time:
15 min

Servings:
4–6

Mama's Grilled and Smothered Chicken

MARINADE:

⅔ cup olive oil

½ cup balsamic vinegar

1 tablespoon liquid smoke

2 teaspoons garlic salt

1 teaspoon crushed dried
    rosemary

½ teaspoon pepper

SMOTHERED CHICKEN:

4–6 boneless, skinless chicken
    breast halves

4 slices bacon

2 tablespoons butter

1 medium onion, sliced

1 cup sliced mushrooms

4–8 slices provolone cheese

MARINADE:

1) Pound chicken breasts, or slice in half
lengthwise.

2) Combine Marinade ingredients in a plastic
zipper bag, and set aside 2 tablespoons for
basting. Place chicken in bag, cover with
Marinade, and seal. Chill 30 minutes, or
up to 2 hours.

SMOTHERED CHICKEN:

1) Cook bacon in a skillet until crisp; remove,
and drain on a paper towel; crumble when
cool. Add butter to bacon drippings, and
sauté onion until caramelized. Using
slotted spoon, remove onion, and set aside.
Sauté mushrooms in skillet until tender;
remove, and set aside.

2) Grill chicken until done. May also pan-
sear or broil.

3) Preheat oven to 350°. Place chicken in
shallow baking dish. Brush both sides
with some reserved marinade; top with
crumbled bacon, mushrooms, and onion.
Bake 5–10 minutes to warm through; top
each piece of chicken with cheese to cover,
and return to oven just long enough to
melt cheese. Serve immediately.

Smoky Mountain Chicken: Marinate
chicken in barbecue sauce. Substitute
thin slices of smoked ham for the bacon,
and omit onions and mushrooms. Pile
several slices of ham loosely on top of
each breast, then top with cheese. Place
in oven just until cheese is melted, and
garnish with sliced green onion before
serving.

| Prep time: | Cook time: | Servings: |
| 10 min | 1 hour | 4–6 |

Picnic Oven-Fried Chicken

This is an excellent make-ahead fried chicken, perfect for packing for a picnic.

3 tablespoons butter

1 cup all-purpose flour

1 teaspoon garlic powder

1 teaspoon Lawry's seasoned salt

2 teaspoons paprika

1 teaspoon Cajun seasoning

1 teaspoon dried thyme

1 tablespoon dried parsley

1 (3- to 4-pound) whole chicken, cut into serving pieces

1) Preheat oven to 425°. Melt butter in 9x13-inch glass baking dish.

2) Whisk together flour with seasonings. Rinse chicken pieces, and dredge in flour mixture; place into baking dish, skin side up, and turn to coat with melted butter. Bake skin side down 35 minutes; turn and bake skin side up another 20–25 minutes, or until juices run clear and chicken is cooked through (internal temperature should reach 175° in the thickest part of thigh, 165° in breast).

3) Transfer to a rack to cool completely. Wrap loosely in paper towels, then place into a large storage bag or container; refrigerate if not using right away.

Prep time:
10 min

Cook time:
1 hour 30 min

Servings:
4–6

Old School Oven Barbecued Chicken

An old-school, low-and-slow way to cook up a barbecue-sauced chicken in the oven—the way that Grandma used to make it.

2 tablespoons olive oil

1 tablespoon butter

1 (3- to 4-pound) whole chicken, cut up

Kosher salt and black pepper to taste

½ medium onion, sliced thin

SAUCE:

1 cup chili sauce or ketchup

1 cup water

2 tablespoons brown sugar

1 teaspoon paprika

⅛ cup apple cider vinegar

2 tablespoons Worcestershire

1 teaspoon Kitchen Bouquet

Dash of liquid smoke (optional)

1 teaspoon hot sauce

Couple dashes dried, red pepper flakes

1 tablespoon yellow mustard (optional)

1) Preheat oven to 325°. Heat olive oil and butter in large skillet over medium heat. Season 1 side of chicken with salt and pepper, placing seasoned side down in skillet. Once in pan, season top; when browned, turn to brown other side. Remove to roasting or baking pan.

2) Add sliced onion to pan drippings, and cook until tender and lightly browned. Deglaze pan with splash of water, scraping up browned bits. Pour over chicken.

3) Whisk together all Sauce ingredients. Pour over chicken and bake, uncovered, basting several times, about 1½ hours, or until juices run clear.

Slow Cooker Method: Remove skin from larger chicken pieces for best results. Follow above directions, except place chicken in slow cooker instead of baking pan. Add onions and Sauce as directed. Cover, and cook on LOW 6–8 hours.

Prep time: 10 min

Cook time: 7 hours

Servings: 4–6

Slow Cooker Rotisserie-Style Chicken

There is a fine line between presentation chicken and falling-off-the-bone chicken when it's cooked in the slow cooker—but the taste is fabulous.

CHICKEN RUB:

2 tablespoons light brown sugar

3 teaspoons kosher salt

¼ teaspoon black pepper

1 teaspoon Cajun seasoning

2 teaspoons paprika

½ teaspoon garlic powder

1 teaspoon onion powder

1 teaspoon herbes de Provence herb blend (rosemary, marjoram, thyme, savory)

CHICKEN:

1 (4- to 5-pound) whole chicken

12 small new or red potatoes

½ cup water

1) Combine ingredients for Rub; set aside.

2) Remove neck and giblets from chicken; save for another use or discard. Season chicken on all sides with Rub, and let rest 15 minutes.

3) Rinse and scrub potatoes, and place in bottom of 6-quart slow cooker. Add water.

4) Fold a long strip of aluminum foil into thirds lengthwise, to create a lift for chicken when it is cooked. Place foil on top of potatoes, put chicken on top, cover, and cook on LOW 7 hours, or HIGH 3–4 hours, or until internal temperature reads 175° in thickest part of thigh.

Cook's Note: For added flavor, season chicken with Rub the night before, and refrigerate overnight.

Brine time:
2 days

Cook time:
30 min

Servings:
4–6

Perfect Southern Fried Chicken

BRINE 1:

1 (3- to 4-pound) whole fryer, cut up

2 tablespoons kosher salt

8–10 ice cubes

BRINE 2:

About 2 cups buttermilk

¼ cup hot sauce

CHICKEN:

2½ cups self-rising flour

1 teaspoon kosher salt

¼ teaspoon black pepper

½ teaspoon Cajun seasoning

½ teaspoon paprika

¼ teaspoon garlic powder

Peanut oil or cooking oil, for frying

2 tablespoons bacon fat, lard, or shortening

Tip: If you don't have a thermometer, oil is generally ready when a pinch of flour tossed in sizzles.

BRINE 1:

1) In large non-metallic bowl, dissolve salt in enough water to cover chicken; stir in ice. Add chicken; cover; refrigerate overnight.

BRINE 2:

1) Next morning, drain, and return chicken to bowl. Cover chicken with buttermilk; mix in hot sauce; cover, and refrigerate until suppertime.

2) Drain chicken in colander 15 minutes, until room temperature.

CHICKEN:

1) In large bowl, whisk flour with all seasonings. Set aside ⅓ cup; coat chicken pieces; place on rack.

2) Fill chicken fryer or cast-iron skillet with enough oil so chicken will completely submerge; add bacon fat.

3) Heat oil to 375°. Fry chicken in small batches, 10–14 minutes. Regulate heat; maintain 375°. Drain on paper towels.

4) For gravy, stir ⅓ cup flour into ⅓ cup frying oil in a skillet over medium heat until browned. Add 2 cups water; bring to a boil; cook and stir until thickened.

Prep time: 15 min

Cook time: 2 hours

Servings: 4–6

Southern-Style Baked Chicken

This method is a favorite in the South for baked chicken. Simply seasoned and delicious, it's one of my husband's favorites.

1 (3- to 5-pound) whole chicken, cut-up

1 tablespoon cooking oil

1 tablespoon melted butter

½ teaspoon seasoned salt

¼ teaspoon onion powder

¼ teaspoon garlic powder

½ teaspoon lemon pepper or black pepper

1 medium onion, halved and sliced

2 large ribs celery, chopped

1 small bell pepper, chopped (optional)

1) Place chicken in a 9x13-inch baking dish, skin side down. Combine oil and butter. Brush chicken, and season with half the seasoned salt, onion powder, garlic powder, and black pepper.

2) Turn chicken skin side up, and season chicken with remaining half of seasonings. Scatter onion, celery, and bell pepper, if desired, on top. Cover tightly, and refrigerate overnight, or a minimum of 30 minutes.

3) Preheat oven to 350°. Bake, covered, 1½ hours; remove, uncover, and continue baking 20–30 minutes more, or until cooked through.

4) Roll chicken in the drippings before transferring to a platter to serve.

Cook's Note: Chicken is done when it reaches 165° for white meat, 175° for dark meat on an instant-read thermometer.

Inactive time
8–12 hours

Cook time:
20 min

Servings:
6–8

Grilled Backyard Barbecued Chicken

One of my favorite grilled foods is backyard barbecued chicken. Mine starts with a brine, gets a nice rub before hitting the grill, and is basted with sauce at the end. Delicious!

1 (3- to 4-pound) whole chicken, cut up

2 tablespoons kosher salt

¼ cup apple cider vinegar

All-Purpose Rub (page 186)

Homemade or commercial bottled barbecue sauce

1) Fill a large pot or container with enough water to cover chicken. Whisk salt into water until dissolved; whisk in vinegar. Add chicken, and refrigerate several hours or overnight.

2) Remove chicken from brine, and allow to drain well. Discard brine.

3) Pat chicken pieces dry, laying out on a platter or baking sheet. Coat chicken well with rub, cover loosely, and refrigerate several hours.

4) Grill chicken, turning occasionally, 12–16 minutes for thighs; 16–20 minutes for legs. Cook breasts, skin side up, for about 10 minutes; turn and cook another 5 minutes, or until juices run clear. Or use an instant-read thermometer: 175° for dark meat, 165° for breasts.

5) Apply barbecue sauce in the last few minutes of cooking.

Chicken and Dumpling Casserole

One of the most popular recipes on DeepSouthDish.com since 2009, this no-stir, layered chicken and dumpling casserole, made with self-rising flour, cream soup, and chicken broth, is reminiscent of the flavor of the real deal, but in a speedy, easy casserole form.

½ stick unsalted butter, melted

3–4 cups cooked shredded chicken

1 cup milk

1 cup self-rising flour

2 cups low-sodium chicken stock or broth

1 (10¾-ounce) can original cream of chicken soup, or 1¼ cups homemade (page 53)

1) Preheat oven to 400°. Pour melted butter into bottom of 9x13-inch baking dish.

2) Layer chicken in bottom of baking dish.

3) In a separate bowl, whisk together milk and flour, and slowly pour over chicken. Do not stir.

4) Whisk together chicken stock and cream of chicken soup. Slowly pour into baking pan. Do not stir.

5) Bake, uncovered, 35–45 minutes, or until top is light golden brown. Let casserole rest before serving.

Chicken Pot Pie Casserole: Add 1–2 (15-ounce) cans mixed veggies, drained, and 1½ cups frozen peas on top of chicken. Finish as above.

Cook's Note: A rotisserie chicken works well. Debone, then boil the bones in water . . . and there's your stock! And you'll have some to freeze for later.

Chicken and Dressing Casserole

Pure comfort food anytime of year, this is a perfect dish to carry to a potluck or church social.

1 pan cornbread, cooked and crumbled (about 6 cups)

4 slices bread, toasted, crumbled

1 medium onion, chopped

1 cup chopped celery

1 stick butter, plus some for top

1 teaspoon each: salt, poultry seasoning, and dried sage

½ teaspoon each: black pepper, marjoram, oregano, rosemary, thyme, and Cajun seasoning

4–6 cups chicken broth

3 eggs, beaten

3 cups cooked, shredded chicken

GRAVY:

½ cup bacon drippings or butter

½ cup all-purpose flour

1–2 cups chicken stock or broth

Salt and black pepper to taste

1) Preheat oven to 350°. Butter a 9x13-inch baking dish; set aside.

2) In a large bowl, combine breads.

3) In a skillet, sauté onion and celery in 1 stick butter; let cool. Add to bread mixture along with seasonings; toss. Add 4 cups broth, and mix well; let stand 5 minutes. (Mixture should resemble cooked oatmeal.) Add beaten eggs; gently toss.

4) Add ½ the dressing to prepared baking dish; top with chicken and remaining dressing, but do not pack down. Dot top with additional butter slices. Bake, uncovered, 40–45 minutes, or until light golden brown. Cook longer for a crunchy consistency on top. Let rest 5–10 minutes before serving.

GRAVY:

1) Heat bacon drippings in a skillet over medium-high heat. Add flour, cooking and stirring constantly with a wooden spoon, until mixture is light brown in color.

2) Reduce heat to medium, slowly stirring in 1 cup stock; add more stock as needed. Season with salt and pepper.

3) Drizzle over individual servings.

Bacon-y Chicken and Rice

Readers of DeepSouthDish.com have loved this recipe from the beginning, and in fact, helped to formulate this version!

5 slices thin-cut bacon

2 (10¾-ounce) cans original cream of chicken soup, or 2½ cups homemade (page 53)

1 cup water

¼ teaspoon garlic salt

Pinch of nutmeg

½ teaspoon Italian seasoning

1½ teaspoons dried parsley

1 cup long-grain rice, uncooked

8 large chicken thighs, or 4 leg quarters, cut up

½ teaspoon kosher salt

½ teaspoon black pepper

¼ teaspoon paprika

¼ teaspoon Cajun seasoning

1) Preheat oven to 300°. Place bacon in single layer in bottom of a glass or ceramic 9x13-inch baking dish, cutting to fit, if needed.

2) Whisk together cream soup, water, garlic salt, nutmeg, Italian seasoning, and parsley.

3) In a separate bowl, blend ⅔ cup soup mixture with rice. Spoon over bacon, and spread evenly.

4) Season chicken on both sides with salt, pepper, paprika, and Cajun seasoning, and place on top of rice mixture, arranging legs in middle, with bone ends turned to center of pan. Pour remaining soup mixture on top.

5) Cover tightly with 2 layers of aluminum foil, and bake 2 hours, without opening oven or peeking.

6) Uncover, check rice for tenderness and chicken for temperature; cover, and return to oven, if needed.

Prep time:
15 min

Cook time:
1 hour 30 mins

Servings:
4–6

Slow-Stewed Southern Chicken

This traditional southern stewed chicken dish begins with a browned, cut-up chicken, that is slow cooked in a roux-based gravy.

1 (3-pound) chicken, cut up

Salt, black pepper, and Cajun seasoning to taste

Up to ½ cup cooking oil

½ cup all-purpose flour

1½ cups chopped onion

½ cup chopped bell pepper

¼ cup chopped celery

2 quarts water, chicken stock, or broth, heated

1 tablespoon minced garlic

Couple dashes hot sauce

2 tablespoons cornstarch

1) Heat oil over medium-high heat in a cast-iron or heavy-bottomed Dutch oven.

2) Season chicken on both sides with salt, pepper, and Cajun seasoning. Cooking in batches, brown chicken on all sides; remove, and set aside.

3) Add oil to pan drippings, if needed, to total ½ cup, and heat over medium-high heat. Add flour, a little at a time, stirring constantly, 4 minutes.

4) Add onion, bell pepper, and celery; cook 3 minutes, then add heated water or broth, a cup at a time, constantly whisking, until well blended. Bring to a boil, reduce heat to low, return chicken to pot, and simmer, uncovered, 1 hour.

5) Add garlic and hot sauce, and cook 30 minutes. Taste, and add additional salt, pepper, and Cajun seasoning, as needed.

6) Remove chicken, and set aside. Skim excess fats, and discard. Prepare a slurry of cornstarch and just enough water to dissolve. Bring broth to a boil, slowly stirring in slurry. Boil, stirring constantly, until mixture is thickened.

Grandma Mac's Chicken Spaghetti

A fresh homemade tomato sauce and a whole cooked hen make for one of my favorite spaghetti dishes in memory of my grandma.

1 (3- to 4-pound) chicken, cut up

3 large tomatoes (1½–2 pounds)

1 (1-pound) package angel hair, vermicelli, or spaghetti

2 tablespoons plus ½ tablespoon olive oil, divided

1 cup chopped onion

¼ cup finely chopped celery

1 teaspoon garlic

1 teaspoon kosher salt

¼ cup chopped fresh basil

1 (8-ounce) can tomato sauce

1 tablespoon sugar

¼ teaspoon dried parsley flakes

¼ teaspoon Italian seasoning

¼ teaspoon Cajun seasoning

¼ teaspoon poultry seasoning

2 bay leaves

1) Boil chicken in salted water to cover until cooked through; set meat aside to cool; reserve 2 cups broth. When cool, debone, shred meat, and discard bones and skin; set aside.

2) Peel tomatoes, and chop, reserving all juice; set aside.

3) Prepare pasta al dente according to package directions. Drain, rinse, drizzle with ½ tablespoon olive oil; set aside.

4) In a skillet, heat 2 tablespoons olive oil over medium heat; add onion, celery, garlic, and salt; sauté 5 minutes or until veggies are tender.

5) Add tomatoes, basil, tomato sauce, sugar, and all seasonings; bring to a boil.

6) Add bay leaves, reduce heat, and simmer 1 hour or until reduced and thickened.

7) Stir in chicken and enough reserved broth until desired consistency is reached; bring back to a boil. Reduce heat, add pasta, and simmer 15–20 minutes, or until heated through.

Chicken, Broccoli, and Rice Casserole

2 tablespoons butter

⅛ cup minced celery

2 tablespoons flour

½ cup milk

½ cup chicken broth

½ cup mayonnaise

1 cup sour cream

¼ teaspoon garlic salt

¼ teaspoon black pepper

¼ teaspoon Cajun seasoning

2 cups cooked rice

3 cups fresh, raw chopped broccoli, blanched

1½ cups grated Cheddar cheese, divided

4 cups shredded cooked chicken

½ cup buttered bread crumbs, crackers, or crumbled potato chips

1) Melt butter in skillet over medium heat. Add celery; cook 2 minutes. Sprinkle in flour; cook and stir 3 minutes. Combine milk and chicken broth; whisk into sauce a little at a time until thickened. Set aside to cool.

2) Preheat oven to 350°. Butter 9x13-inch baking pan. Whisk mayonnaise and sour cream into cooled sauce. Mix in garlic salt, pepper, and Cajun seasoning.

3) Add rice, broccoli, 1 cup cheese, and chicken. Mix well, and turn into baking pan.

4) Bake uncovered, 30 minutes, or till cooked through. Remove; add crumb topping and remaining ½ cup cheese on top. Return to oven; bake another 10 minutes or until topping browns and cheese melts. Let sit a few minutes before serving.

Cook's Notes: Omit chicken to make a simple Broccoli and Rice Casserole, or omit rice for a Cheesy Chicken and Broccoli dish. May substitute 2 (10-ounce) packages frozen broccoli, thawed and drained.

Prep time: 15 min

Cook time: 35 min

Servings: 4–6

Chicken and Biscuits

This casserole is a variation of our traditional pot pie with a topping of biscuits. Use my buttermilk biscuit recipe (page 28), or substitute refrigerated or thawed, frozen biscuits.

18 biscuits, homemade, frozen and thawed, or refrigerated

¼ cup unsalted butter

½ cup chopped onion

½ cup chopped carrots

¼ cup chopped celery

1 teaspoon minced garlic

⅓ cup all-purpose flour

4 cups chicken broth

1 cup half-and-half

4 cups chopped, cooked chicken

½ cup frozen peas, thawed

¼ teaspoon crushed dried thyme

¼ teaspoon crushed dried rosemary

⅛ teaspoon poultry seasoning

¼ teaspoon Cajun seasoning

Salt and pepper to taste

1) Butter a 9x13-inch baking dish; set aside. Allow biscuits to come to room temperature. Preheat oven to 350°.

2) Melt butter in a skillet over medium heat; sauté onion, carrots, and celery until tender, about 5 minutes, stirring constantly. Add garlic, and cook 1 minute.

3) Sprinkle in flour, cooking and stirring 3 minutes. Slowly add broth; bring to boil, then simmer 5 minutes, until thickened.

4) Stir in half-and-half, bring heat up, and cook until heated through. Add chicken, peas, and seasonings.

5) Transfer hot mixture immediately to prepared baking dish, and quickly top with biscuits. Bake, uncovered, 20–30 minutes, or until bubbly, and biscuits are browned and cooked through.

Cook's Notes: For biscuits to cook through, they must be placed on hot filling. Substitute a rotisserie chicken, but be mindful of their additional salt.

Southern Poppy Seed Chicken Casserole

Cream soups are standard in what is probably considered to be "the" southern chicken casserole for ages . . . and remains a popular and beloved dish.

1 (10¾-ounce) can original cream of chicken soup, or 1¼ cups homemade (page 53)

1 (10¾-ounce) can cream of mushroom soup, or 1¼ cups homemade (page 53)

1 cup sour cream

1 cup chicken broth

4 cups chopped or shredded, cooked chicken

1½ sleeves saltine or Ritz crackers

½ tablespoon poppy seeds

½ cup (1 stick) unsalted butter, melted

1) Preheat oven to 350°. Butter a 9x13-inch baking dish; set aside.

2) In a large bowl, whisk together soups, sour cream, and chicken broth. Add other seasonings, if desired; set aside.

3) Place chicken in prepared dish, and pour in soup mixture.

4) In a separate small bowl, crumble crackers, stir in poppy seeds, and mix with melted butter; spread on top of casserole. Bake, uncovered, 35–40 minutes, or until casserole is bubbly and cracker topping has browned.

5) Remove, and let rest 5 minutes before serving. May be served as is, or spooned over cooked rice or noodles.

Seafood

Prep time: 15 min

Cook time: 15–30 min

Servings: 4–6

Seafood Stuffing Mix/Seafood Cakes

A versatile stuffing mix made with toasted bread, sautéed onion, and sweet bell pepper, tossed with crab and shrimp, and versatile enough for use in many different recipes.

4 tablespoons butter

1 cup finely minced Vidalia or other sweet onion

¼ cup finely minced green bell pepper

4 slices white or white wheat bread, toasted

1 large egg

Pinch of kosher salt

¼ teaspoon black pepper

¼–½ teaspoon Cajun seasoning

½ teaspoon Old Bay Seasoning

Couple shakes dried parsley

1 pound crabmeat, picked through for shells

½ pound raw shrimp, peeled, deveined, and chopped (optional)

1) Melt butter in large skillet over medium heat; add onion and green pepper, and cook until softened. Remove from heat, and set aside to cool slightly.

2) Toast bread slices, sprinkle each piece with a good spray of water, and set aside in a bowl about 2 minutes.

3) Squeeze bread, and break it up. Add egg, and mix. Add salt, pepper, Cajun seasoning, Old Bay, parsley, and sautéed onion and bell pepper; mix well.

4) Gently mix in shrimp and crab. Use as desired to stuff shrimp, crab shells, or flounder; to make crab patties for po'boys; as a filling for squash, eggplant, or other vegetables; or to form crab cakes or bite-size crab balls (next page).

Cook's Note: To easily pick out any shell, spread crab on baking sheet in a single layer, and place in a 200° oven for 3 minutes. The shell will be visible and easy to pick out.

SEAFOOD

Seafood Stuffing Mix continued

HOW TO USE SEAFOOD STUFFING MIX:

1) **Gulf Coast Style Pan-Fried Crab Cakes:** Prepare Seafood Stuffing Mix omitting shrimp. Heat 1 tablespoon cooking oil with 1 tablespoon butter in a skillet over medium to medium-high heat. Form into 8 patties. Pan-fry on both sides. Serve with Comeback Dressing (page 70).

2) **Stuffed Shrimp:** Select 18–24, jumbo shrimp, peeled, but with tail tip intact, deveined, butterflied, and rinsed. Preheat oven to 375°. Spray a large sheet pan with nonstick cooking spray, and set aside. Using approximately 1 tablespoon for each shrimp, form stuffing mix into small oblong shaped bullets, and press firmly into butterflied shrimp. Bake 20 minutes. Melt 2 tablespoons butter, and drizzle on top.

3) **Crabmeat and Cheese Po'boy:** Line a baking sheet with parchment or wax paper, and set aside. Form stuffing mix into thin, oval patties. Dredge patties in ¼ cup flour, lightly coating on both sides. Refrigerate 30 minutes or longer; may also freeze at this point. Heat 2 tablespoons cooking oil in a large skillet, and brown patties until crisp on both sides, adding additional oil as needed. Split French bread lengthwise, butter, and toast. Dress with mayonnaise, cheese, crabmeat patties, and top half of bread; place into skillet, using a spatula to press down on po'boy as it toasts. Flip, and press until nicely toasted and cheese is melted. Remove, and dress with sliced tomato, shredded lettuce, and sliced pickles, or with a pickle spear on the side. Serve immediately.

4) **Stuffed Flounder:** Preheat oven to 350°. Line a large baking pan with nonstick foil. Cut a slit lengthwise head to tail, down the dark side of 4–6 (1-pound) whole flounder, cleaned; make pockets on both sides of slit, using a sharp fillet knife to cut along the back bone to upper and lower fins, without cutting through. Sprinkle flounder with salt and pepper, and stuff, then place onto prepared pan. Squeeze lemon juice over top, and drizzle with 2 tablespoons melted butter. Bake, uncovered, 30 minutes, or until fish flakes easily, basting with additional 2 tablespoons melted butter halfway through. Place tray under broiler just long enough to brown top of stuffing. Serve with wedges of lemon on the side and a generous side salad.

Prep time:
10 min

Cook time:
35 mins

Servings:
6–8

Gulf Coast Crab and Rice

Crab and rice was once a popular dish on The Point where my mama grew up, and where seafood was central to every family, including ours since my poppy was a fisherman. All forms of seafood dishes—from fish, shrimp, crabs, and oysters—were inexpensive and common. Today, the seafood industry is much smaller and the costs higher, but seafood is still very much central to our lives here on the coast, and this dish is one of my favorites.

1 pound fresh crabmeat

2 tablespoons unsalted butter

1 cup chopped onion

½ cup chopped green bell pepper

¼ cup chopped celery

1 tablespoon minced garlic

1 (1-pound) can whole tomatoes, cut up, undrained

3 cups water

1 cup long-grain rice

1 teaspoon dried parsley

½ teaspoon dried oregano

1 teaspoon ground coriander

½ teaspoon Old Bay Seasoning (optional)

1 teaspoon Cajun seasoning

1 teaspoon kosher salt

½ teaspoon black pepper

Couple dashes hot sauce

2 small bay leaves

1) Drain crabmeat, reserving any juices. Pick through crab for any stray shell; set aside.

2) Heat butter in large saucepan; sauté onion, bell pepper, and celery until tender, about 4 minutes. Add garlic; cook 1 minute.

3) Add remaining ingredients, including juices from crab, except crabmeat; mix well. Bring to a boil, reduce heat to low, and simmer until most liquid has been absorbed, 20–25 minutes. Remove from heat, gently fold in crab, cover, and let rest 5 minutes. Discard bay leaves.

4) Spoon into bowls. Pass hot sauce at the table.

Cajun Crabmeat au Gratin

A well-loved dish here in the Deep South, this is also delicious with shrimp or crawfish. Pass under the broiler for a crunchy top.

1 pound lump crabmeat

4 tablespoons butter

¼ cup sliced green onions

4 tablespoons all-purpose flour

½ teaspoon kosher salt

¼ teaspoon black pepper

½ teaspoon Cajun seasoning

½ teaspoon Old Bay Seasoning

½ teaspoon chopped fresh parsley

Pinch of dry mustard

2 cups half-and-half

4 tablespoons dry white wine

2½ cups shredded sharp Cheddar cheese, divided

2 tablespoons butter, melted

¼ cup dry bread crumbs (optional)

1) Drain crabmeat, and pick through for shell; set aside. Preheat oven to 350°. Butter au gratin dishes, individual ramekins, or a small casserole dish; set aside.

2) Melt 4 tablespoons butter in medium-size skillet over medium heat; add onions, and sauté 1 minute.

3) Sprinkle in flour, a little at a time. Add seasonings. Stir in half-and-half and wine, and remove from heat.

4) Divide crabmeat evenly between dishes; divide 2 cups Cheddar cheese on top, then evenly divide sauce among dishes.

5) Sprinkle tops with remaining ½ cup cheese, then bread crumbs, if desired. Bake 15–20 minutes, or until bubbly.

Gulf Coast Shrimp and Grits

2 pounds small to medium shrimp, peeled and deveined

1 cup chopped andouille sausage

3 tablespoons cooking oil, divided

1 tablespoon unsalted butter

1 tablespoon all-purpose flour

½ cup chopped onion

¼ cup chopped green bell pepper

⅛ cup chopped celery

1 (10-ounce) can diced tomatoes and green chiles, drained

3 teaspoons Cajun seasoning

1½ cups shrimp stock or chicken broth

Kosher salt and black pepper to taste

Red pepper flakes (optional)

Prepared Creamy Southern Garlic Cheese Grits (page 48)

Sliced green onion, for garnish

1) Pat shrimp dry with paper towels. (Reserve heads and shells to make stock, if desired.)

2) In skillet over medium heat, sauté sausage in 1 tablespoon cooking oil. Remove sausage, and set aside. To same skillet, add shrimp and cook just until pink. Remove, and set aside with sausage.

3) In pan drippings, add remaining 2 tablespoons cooking oil and butter. Stir in flour; cook and stir 3–4 minutes or until lightly browned. Add onion, bell pepper, celery, tomatoes, and Cajun seasoning; cook and stir 3–5 minutes. Slowly stir in stock, and bring to a boil; reduce heat, and simmer 10 minutes.

4) Add shrimp and sausage back to skillet, and heat through. To thicken sauce, stir in additional butter, if desired; add salt and pepper. Sprinkle with red pepper flakes, if desired.

5) Spoon Garlic Cheese Grits into serving bowl, top with several spoons of shrimp mixture, and garnish bowls with sliced green onion.

Classic Southern Fried Shrimp

Self-rising flour contains baking powder, which gives a more crisp and crunchy result than all-purpose flour.

1 pound raw medium shrimp
1 large egg
1 cup milk
2 cups self-rising flour
1 teaspoon Cajun seasoning
½ teaspoon Old Bay Seasoning
½ teaspoon kosher salt
¼–½ teaspoon black pepper
1 teaspoon lemon pepper

1) Preheat deep fryer or heat oil in a large heavy pot to 350°. Peel and devein shrimp, rinsing well. Pat dry with paper towels.

2) Whisk together egg and milk, and add shrimp to mixture.

3) In separate bowl, stir flour together with all seasonings. Dip shrimp in flour mixture to coat, then place in colander set over a plate or tray. Toss shrimp in flour mixture a second time, place back in colander, and shake well to remove excess flour.

4) Fry in small batches, 3–4 minutes per batch, or until golden brown. Shake fryer basket, and turn out onto a platter lined with paper towels, then sprinkle with just a bit of additional salt.

Batter Fried: Add ½ cup flour along with 2 tablespoons melted and cooled butter, to beaten egg and milk. Dip shrimp in batter, shake off to drain, then roll in seasoned flour before frying.

Seasoned-To-Perfection Shrimp Boil

This works with live crabs and crawfish, presoaked in salted water.

1 extra large onion, peeled and quartered

3 large garlic cloves, peeled and smashed

½ cup vegetable oil

½ cup ketchup

Couple dashes hot sauce

1 teaspoon black pepper

1 tablespoon Cajun seasoning

2 large lemons, sliced

¼ cup white vinegar

3 tablespoons liquid crab boil

½ (1-pound) bag loose crab boil, divided (optional)

1 pound andouille or other spicy smoked sausage, cut into 3-inch lengths

10 new or small red potatoes

4 ears corn, shucked and cleaned, cut into thirds

3–5 pounds (16- to 20-count) shrimp, shells and heads intact, rinsed

1 cup kosher salt

1) Fill a 6-quart stockpot halfway with water, and bring to a boil, using about 1 quart water per pound shrimp. Add first 9 ingredients; return to a boil.

2) Add crab boil(s), sausage, and potatoes; boil 10 minutes. Add corn, and boil 5 minutes, then add shrimp; immediately remove from heat.

3) Add salt; stir well to dissolve. Cover pot, and allow to soak about 10 minutes—more for jumbo shrimp, 3–5 minutes for small. (For crabs, bring back to a boil, then add crabs, and cook 15–18 minutes.)

4) Remove shrimp with slotted spoon to a platter, along with corn, potatoes, and sausage. Sprinkle with more loose crab boil, if desired.

SEAFOOD

Shrimp Boat Spaghetti

This dish gets its name from being cooked on a shrimp boat. All the ingredients are easily transported on a shrimp boat, then they add a scoop out of the day's catch.

1 pound medium shrimp, peeled and deveined

½ teaspoon Cajun seasoning

1 tablespoon olive oil

1 cup chopped Vidalia or yellow onion

½ cup chopped medium sweet bell pepper (red or green)

2 garlic cloves, chopped

1 (14.5-ounce) can Italian-style stewed tomatoes

1 (26.5-ounce) can your favorite spaghetti sauce

2 medium bay leaves

½ teaspoon dried basil

2–3 very generous pinches kosher salt

1 (1-pound) package spaghetti noodles

Freshly cracked black pepper and parsley flakes to garnish

1) Rinse shrimp; drain well, and pat dry with paper towels. Spread out on a large baking pan in a single layer, and sprinkle with Cajun seasoning. Set aside.

2) Add olive oil to a deep skillet, and heat to medium. Add onion and bell pepper, and sauté until tender. Add garlic, and sauté 1 more minute.

3) Add stewed tomatoes, and mash. Simmer 10–15 minutes. Add spaghetti sauce, bay leaves, and basil; simmer 15 minutes.

4) Bring a large pot of water to a boil, adding salt. Add pasta, and cook to al dente. Drain, reserving 1 cup pasta water; set aside.

5) Add shrimp to sauce; stir well, and cook just until pink. Add only enough reserved pasta water to sauce, as needed, if sauce becomes too thick.

6) Add several spoons of sauce to pasta, and toss well.

7) To serve, plate pasta, top with sauce, crack a bit of fresh black pepper on top, and sprinkle lightly with parsley.

Prep time: 15 min

Cook time: 40 min

Servings: 4–6

Shrimp Pasta in Tomato Cream Sauce

6 ounces bowtie pasta

1 tablespoon olive oil

2 tablespoons butter, divided

1 pound (31- to 35-count) medium wild caught American shrimp, peeled, deveined, and seasoned to taste with kosher salt, black pepper, Old Bay Seasoning, and Cajun seasoning

1 cup chopped onion

1 tablespoon minced garlic

2 (15-ounce) cans stewed tomatoes, chopped, undrained or 2 cups peeled, chopped fresh tomatoes, juices retained

1 (8-ounce) can tomato sauce

1 teaspoon kosher salt

¼ teaspoon black pepper

¼ teaspoon Cajun seasoning

1 teaspoon sugar

½ cup heavy cream

1 tablespoon chopped fresh parsley

1 tablespoon chopped fresh basil, plus more, for garnish

Freshly grated Parmesan cheese

1) Boil pasta in a large pot of well-salted water to al dente, about 12 minutes. Drain, reserving ½ cup pasta water.

2) Heat olive oil with 1 tablespoon butter in a large skillet over medium-high heat, until bubbly. Sauté seasoned shrimp, stirring regularly, until opaque. Remove with slotted spoon, and set aside.

3) Add onion to skillet, and cook until lightly browned; add garlic, and cook 1 minute.

4) Stir in tomatoes and sauce; add salt, pepper, Cajun seasoning, and sugar. Bring to a boil, reduce heat, and simmer 20 minutes.

5) Stir in cream until warmed through, return shrimp to skillet, and add remaining 1 tablespoon butter. Add pasta, parsley, and basil; toss until warmed through.

6) Add some reserved pasta water to thin sauce, if needed. Transfer to bowl, top with Parmesan, and garnish with additional chopped basil, if desired.

Shrimp Creole

Fresh Gulf shrimp, cooked in a spicy Creole tomato sauce and served over a bed of hot steaming rice.

SEAFOOD

1 pound (31- to 35-count) medium shrimp, peeled and deveined

1 tablespoon olive oil

1 tablespoon unsalted butter

1 medium onion, chopped

1 small green bell pepper, chopped

1 stalk celery, chopped

1 (28-ounce) can crushed tomatoes

½ teaspoon kosher salt

¼ teaspoon cayenne pepper

2 garlic cloves, minced

1 bay leaf

1 tablespoon all-purpose flour

2 tablespoons water

½ teaspoon Cajun seasoning

Couple dashes Worcestershire

Couple dashes hot sauce to taste (optional)

1 green onion, sliced

1 tablespoon chopped fresh parsley

1) Rinse shrimp, pat dry with paper towels, and set aside.

2) In a large skillet, heat olive oil and butter over medium heat. Add chopped onion, green bell pepper, and celery; sauté until tender, about 5 minutes. Add tomatoes, salt, cayenne pepper, garlic, and bay leaf; bring to a boil. Reduce heat to medium low, and simmer for 30 minutes, or until reduced and thickened.

3) Make a slurry of flour and water, and stir into skillet. Continue cooking another 5 minutes.

4) Sprinkle shrimp with Cajun seasoning, and add to skillet with Worcestershire and hot sauce. Cook 5–6 minutes, or until opaque.

5) Stir in green onion and parsley. Serve over hot, steamed rice.

Mama's Shrimp and Fettuccine

Mama's handwritten recipe said, "This dish will make them scream for more."

1 pound medium shrimp, peeled, deveined, and rinsed

1 pound fettuccine

2 tablespoons olive oil, divided

½ cup diced tasso, ham, andouille, or other smoked sausage

4 green onions, sliced

1 (14-ounce) can artichokes, drained and quartered

1 (2-ounce) jar chopped pimentos, drained

1 teaspoon chopped fresh thyme

1 teaspoon chopped fresh oregano

½ teaspoon paprika

¼ teaspoon garlic powder

¼–½ teaspoon Cajun seasoning

Kosher salt and black pepper to taste

½ stick unsalted butter

Red pepper flakes to taste

1) Pat shrimp dry with paper towels; set aside. Cook pasta per package directions; drain; reserve 2 cups pasta water.

2) Heat 1 tablespoon olive oil in large skillet, and cook ham or sausage until seared; use a slotted spoon to remove, and set aside.

3) Add last 1 tablespoon oil to skillet; sear shrimp; remove; set aside with sausage.

4) Add green onions to skillet; cook and stir 1 minute. Add artichokes and pimentos; cook and stir until warmed through.

5) Return meat and shrimp to pan; add herbs and seasonings. Add butter, stirring until melted. Stir in some reserved pasta water, a little at a time, until desired thickness.

6) Add drained pasta, and toss to coat. Sprinkle with red pepper flakes, and serve immediately with a side salad and bread.

Crawfish Pasta

A Jazz Fest favorite, spicy crawfish are cooked in a rich and creamy sauce and served with pasta.

1 pound dry rotini pasta

1 stick butter

5 medium cloves garlic, finely minced

2 green onions, sliced

2 cups half-and-half

1 teaspoon to 2 tablespoons Cajun seasoning

1 pound fresh, cooked or frozen Louisiana crawfish tails, undrained

Parsley to taste

Kosher salt and black pepper to taste

1) Cook pasta al dente, according to package directions. Rinse, and drain well; set aside.

2) Melt butter, and sauté garlic 2 minutes. Add green onion, and cook 2 minutes. Stir in half-and-half and Cajun seasoning, a little at a time, to desired taste. Cook over medium heat 5 minutes.

3) Add crawfish with juices, and cook 5–10 minutes, or until nicely thickened and heated through. Stir in pasta; add parsley, salt, and pepper.

4) Serve immediately, or hold over very low heat an additional 10 minutes, stirring occasionally.

5) Serve with hot French bread.

Crawfish Étouffée

Crawfish, simmered in a very simple butter roux, and finished with a little fresh parsley and green onion. Serve over hot rice with fresh French bread for dipping.

½ stick unsalted butter

¼ cup all-purpose flour

1 cup chopped onion

½ cup chopped green bell pepper

¼ cup chopped celery

2 teaspoons minced garlic

2 cups seafood stock or chicken broth

1 teaspoon kosher salt

Black pepper to taste

¼–½ teaspoon Cajun seasoning

1 pound fresh, cooked, or frozen Louisiana crawfish tails, with fat

1 tablespoon chopped fresh parsley, plus extra, for garnish

¼ cup sliced green onion, plus extra, for garnish

1) Melt butter in a large skillet over medium heat; add flour, and stir 4 minutes or until caramel colored.

2) Add onions, bell pepper, and celery; cook 3–4 minutes or until tender. Add garlic, and cook 1 minute.

3) Slowly stir in stock or broth. Add salt, pepper, and Cajun seasoning. Bring mixture to a boil; reduce heat to a medium low, cover, and simmer 15 minutes, stirring occasionally.

4) Add crawfish with juices; cook and stir until heated through. Stir in parsley and green onion, reserving a bit for garnish.

5) Serve immediately over hot, cooked rice with fresh French bread and a side salad.

Trout with Crab and Shrimp Stuffing

4 (10-ounce) speckled trout, dressed, heads, tails removed

STUFFING:

2 tablespoons butter

¼ cup finely minced yellow onion

¼ cup finely minced celery

8 (20-count) shrimp, roughly chopped

¼ teaspoon each: Cajun seasoning, Old Bay Seasoning, and black pepper

Pinch of kosher salt

1 teaspoon chopped fresh parsley

2 tablespoons mayonnaise

1 teaspoon fresh lemon juice

¼ cup plain, dry bread crumbs

4 ounces lump crab, picked

DREDGE:

1 cup self-rising flour

½ cup cornmeal

½ teaspoon each: kosher salt and black pepper

1 large egg, beaten

¼ cup milk

2 cups vegetable oil

STUFFING:

1) In a large skillet, melt butter until lightly browned; add onion and celery; cook 2 minutes. Add shrimp, and cook until opaque. Remove from heat; cool slightly.

2) Combine seasonings, mayonnaise, lemon juice, and bread crumbs; fold in crab. Stuff trout; secure with toothpick, if desired.

DREDGE:

1) Combine flour, cornmeal, salt, and pepper in pie plate.

2) In separate pie plate, beat egg and milk. Dip each trout into egg mixture, then in flour mixture, coating both sides.

3) Fry trout on each side 4–6 minutes, until golden brown and crispy. Transfer to a rack placed over a tray, to drain. Serve immediately with lemon wedges and your favorite sauce.

Baked Fish

Works well with many types of fish, including catfish, flounder, cod, halibut, perch, tilapia, and other similar white fish.

4–6 large speckled trout fillets or other white fish

1 teaspoon kosher salt

¼ teaspoon black pepper

1 teaspoon Old Bay Seasoning

1 teaspoon Cajun seasoning

1 tablespoon olive oil

¼ cup unsalted butter, melted

1 lemon, zested, and cut into wedges

1 tablespoon sliced green onion

2 teaspoons chopped fresh parsley

Cook's Notes: If you're using frozen fish, cover in milk, and refrigerate 1 hour to freshen it before cooking.

1) Preheat oven to 375°. Brush a foil-lined baking sheet with olive oil. Drain fish, pat dry, and place onto baking sheet.

2) In a small bowl, combine salt, pepper, Old Bay, and Cajun seasoning; set aside.

3) Mix 1 tablespoon olive oil with melted butter. Brush trout with ½ the olive oil-butter blend. Sprinkle seasoning mixture evenly on top.

4) Zest lemon on top of fish, and bake, uncovered, 8–10 minutes per inch of thickness, or until fish is mostly opaque throughout, and flakes easily—taking care not to overcook. Drizzle reserved olive oil-butter mixture on top of fillets, then sprinkle with green onion and parsley. Squeeze juice from zested lemon all over fillets; serve immediately with additional fresh lemon wedges, if desired.

| Prep time: 10 min | Cook time: 5 min | Servings: 4–6 |

Southern Fried Catfish

A true Deep South favorite served regularly at my house on Fridays.

3 pounds catfish fillets

Kosher salt and black pepper to taste

¼–½ teaspoon Cajun seasoning

½ teaspoon Old Bay Seasoning (optional)

½ cup self-rising flour

2 cups all-purpose yellow cornmeal

Cooking oil, for frying

1) Rinse fillets, and pat dry. May cut each fillet into 3–4 strips, if desired. Season fish on both sides with salt, pepper, Cajun seasoning, and Old Bay. Let fillets rest while heating fryer to 375°.

2) Whisk together flour and cornmeal in a large bowl. Dip fillets in mixture until well coated; shake off excess; set aside.

3) Gently drop fillets into heated fryer with basket lowered, a few at a time so as not to overcrowd them. Fry 4–6 minutes, or until fish floats and is golden brown. Drain on several layers of paper towels before transferring to platter or individual plates.

Prep time: 5 min

Inactive time: 3–4 hours

Yield: About 1¼ cups

Cocktail Sauce

1 cup chili sauce

¼ cup prepared horseradish

Juice of 1 lemon

Couple dashes hot sauce

Pinch of kosher salt

¼ teaspoon black pepper

1) Combine all ingredients well.

2) Refrigerate 3–4 hours before using.

Homemade Chili Sauce

Since I use chili sauce in a lot of dishes, I decided to make a homemade version. It's just to my liking, and much cheaper than the store-bought variety!

1 (8-ounce) can tomato sauce

2 tablespoons tomato paste

Juice of ½ lemon

2 tablespoons light brown sugar

¼ teaspoon dry mustard

¼ teaspoon onion powder

¼ teaspoon garlic powder

¼ teaspoon chili powder

Couple dashes Worcestershire

1) Whisk ingredients together until thoroughly mixed.

2) Refrigerate 3–4 hours before using.

Beef & Pork

Mississippi Roast

Mississippi Roast, made using a rump or chuck roast and a few convenience products, has become one of the favorite Sunday roasts from readers at DeepSouthDish.com. It produces a moist, tender, and delicious roast with a wonderful gravy and a nice spicy bite.

1 (3- to 5-pound) boneless beef rump or chuck roast

3 garlic cloves, cut into slivers

Black pepper to taste

1 tablespoon bacon drippings, or vegetable oil

1 stalk celery, cut into chunks

1 medium-size onion, halved and sliced

1 envelope dry ranch dressing mix

1 envelope dry brown gravy or au jus mix

½ teaspoon crushed dried thyme

½ teaspoon crushed dried rosemary

1 cup Coca-Cola Classic

1 large bay leaf

1 whole jalapeño (I use pickled)

4 golden peperoncini peppers

1 tablespoon unsalted butter

1 tablespoon cornstarch

1) Cut small slits all over roast, and insert a garlic sliver into each cut.

2) Season roast on both sides with black pepper. Heat bacon drippings or oil in large skillet, and brown roast on both sides.

3) Add celery chunks to bottom of 6-quart slow cooker, and place roast on top. Add onion to skillet, and cook 3 minutes. Transfer to top of roast.

4) Combine ranch dressing mix, gravy mix, thyme, and rosemary. Add Coke, and whisk until well blended; set aside.

5) Add bay leaf, jalapeño, and peperoncini to top of roast, and pour Coke mixture over top. Cover, and cook on LOW 7–8 hours, or on HIGH 4–5 hours.

6) To thicken gravy, remove roast from slow cooker, and keep warm. Discard jalapeño. Carefully transfer juices to a saucepan, reserving peperoncini. Stir in butter. Make a slurry of cornstarch and water. Whisk into juices, and bring to a boil; reduce heat, and simmer until thickened. Purée reserved peperoncini, and return to pot.

7) Serve roast sliced with gravy.

Atlanta Brisket

1 (3- to 5-pound) beef brisket

1 (12-ounce) can Coca-Cola Classic

1 (12-ounce) bottle chili sauce, or 1 batch homemade (page 160)

1 envelope dry onion soup mix

1 teaspoon liquid smoke (optional)

Kosher salt, black pepper, and Cajun seasoning to taste

½ Vidalia or other sweet onion, sliced

1 tablespoon cornstarch

Cook's Notes: Brisket may be prepared ahead, sliced, and stored in sauce, covered, and refrigerated. To reheat, skim off additional hardened fat, cover, and heat in preheated 350° oven for 45 minutes.

1) Place brisket into a large zipper bag or glass baking pan for marinating. Whisk together Coke, chili sauce, and dry onion soup mix; pour over brisket. Refrigerate 8 hours or overnight, turning several times.

2) Preheat oven to 325°. Remove brisket from marinade, reserving marinade in refrigerator. Rub liquid smoke into lean side of brisket, and season lightly with salt, pepper, and Cajun seasoning; rub in.

3) Place brisket, fat side up, on foil large enough to wrap; cut several knife slices into the fat cap. Top with onion and reserved marinade; seal foil.

4) Bake 1 hour per pound, rotating pan occasionally. Remove from oven, and carefully open to check internal temperature (should be 180°); re-seal foil, and let rest 30 minutes.

5) Transfer brisket to cutting board. Skim fat from sauce; transfer sauce to large skillet; add reserved marinade. Boil 4 minutes.

6) Whisk together cornstarch with enough water to make a slurry, and slowly stir into sauce, stirring constantly, until thickened and smooth.

7) Slice brisket across grain, place on a large platter, and pour sauce over top.

BEEF & PORK

Prep time: 10 min

Cook time: 15 min

Servings: 4–6

Chicken-Fried Steak with Milk Gravy

Cube steaks, dredged in seasoned flour, fried in fat and bacon drippings, and drizzled with a peppered milk gravy for a classic southern favorite.

BEEF & PORK

½ cup vegetable oil

2 tablespoons bacon fat

2 cups self-rising flour

1½ teaspoons seasoned salt

¼ teaspoon black pepper

¼ teaspoon garlic powder

1 cup milk

2 large eggs

6 cube steaks

¼–½ teaspoon Cajun seasoning

GRAVY:

2 tablespoons butter, along with pan drippings to equal ¼ cup

1½–2 cups milk, as needed

Salt and black pepper to taste

1) Heat oil and bacon fat in heavy skillet over medium-high heat.

2) In a medium bowl, whisk together flour, seasoned salt, pepper, and garlic powder; reserve ¼ cup.

3) In separate bowl, beat milk with eggs.

4) Season cube steaks with Cajun seasoning, and pound in. Dredge in seasoned flour, shake off excess, dip in egg wash, then back in flour.

5) Carefully add meat in batches to hot oil in skillet, making sure it does not stick. Cook until browned, 3–4 minutes per side.

GRAVY:

1) Melt butter in pan drippings; sprinkle in reserved ¼ cup seasoned flour. Cook to light blond color, stirring constantly, and scraping up browned bits from bottom.

2) Whisk in 1½ cups milk; bring to a boil, and cook over medium heat, stirring constantly, until thickened. Add more milk, as needed. Season with salt and pepper.

3) Serve steaks with gravy spooned over top.

Salisbury Steak with Mushroom Gravy

This diner classic takes a shortcut with mushroom soup for gravy.

1½ pounds ground beef

½ cup Italian-style bread crumbs

1 large egg, beaten

¼ cup minced onion

Couple dashes Worcestershire

2 (10¾-ounce) cans cream of mushroom soup, or 2½ cups homemade (page 53), divided

¼ teaspoon Cajun seasoning or seasoned salt

2 tablespoons bacon fat, or vegetable oil

Couple dashes Kitchen Bouquet browning sauce (optional)

2 cups sliced fresh mushrooms

Italian Style: Replace soup and Kitchen Bouquet with mixture of 2 (14½-ounce) cans Italian-style diced tomatoes mixed with 1 (8-ounce) can tomato sauce.

1) Combine ground beef, bread crumbs, egg, onion, Worcestershire, and ¼ cup soup. Shape into 6 oval patties; sprinkle both sides with Cajun seasoning or seasoned salt.

2) Heat bacon fat in 12-inch skillet over medium-high heat. Add patties in 2 batches, browning on both sides, turning carefully. Transfer to a platter; set aside. Drain off excess fat from skillet.

3) Add remaining soup to skillet, and bring to a boil; reduce heat; stir in Kitchen Bouquet and mushrooms; cover, and cook 2–3 minutes, or until mushrooms release their liquid.

4) Return patties to skillet, turning to coat both sides; cover, and cook over medium low, turning several times, 30 minutes, or until patties are no longer pink.

5) Serve patties with gravy and mushrooms spooned over the top.

BEEF & PORK

Hamburger Steak with Onion Gravy

PATTIES:

3 tablespoons vegetable oil

1½ pounds 80/20 ground chuck

¾ cup finely chopped onion

1 large egg

1 teaspoon seasoned salt

½ teaspoon garlic powder

¼–½ teaspoon black pepper

⅓ cup all-purpose flour

GRAVY:

1 large onion, halved and sliced

1 cup beef broth

¼ cup all-purpose flour

¼ teaspoon seasoned salt

¼ teaspoon black pepper

½ tablespoon Worcestershire

1 teaspoon Kitchen Bouquet
   (optional)

PATTIES:

1) Heat oil over medium-high heat in large heavy-bottomed stainless skillet.

2) In a medium-size bowl, combine ground chuck, onion, egg, seasoned salt, garlic powder, and pepper. Shape into 4–6 equal-size patties. Dip each patty into flour, and cook in skillet until browned on both sides; remove, and set aside.

GRAVY:

1) Add sliced onion to pan drippings in skillet, and cook over medium heat until lightly caramelized, stirring regularly.

1) Combine broth with 1 cup water; whisk in flour, seasoned salt, and pepper. Pour into skillet with onion, and stir constantly until mixture begins to thicken. Add Worcestershire and Kitchen Bouquet.

2) Return patties to skillet, turning to coat, and reduce heat to low. Simmer, covered, 20 minutes.

3) Serve with mashed potatoes and green beans, or a mixed garden salad on the side.

Slow Cooker Beef Tips and Rice

Braising beef, cut into meaty chunks, slow cooked in a well-seasoned gravy and served over rice or egg noodles is as good as it gets!

1 (3- to 5-pound) braising roast* (see note)

Black pepper to taste

½ teaspoon Cajun seasoning

1 tablespoon cooking oil

½ cup beef broth

1½ cups water

Splash of red wine (optional)

1 envelope brown gravy mix

¼ teaspoon dried thyme

Dash of Worcestershire

Dash of hot sauce

1 tablespoon cornstarch (optional)

*Use a braising type of roast for this recipe. You'll want an eye or bottom round (not top round) or a chuck (shoulder, arm, or blade) roast.

1) Cut meat into large cubes, and season with black pepper and Cajun seasoning.

2) Heat oil in a cast-iron skillet over medium-high heat. Sear meat until browned; transfer to slow cooker.

3) Add beef broth to skillet, and deglaze, scraping up browned bits. Transfer to slow cooker.

4) Whisk together water, wine, if desired, brown gravy mix, thyme, Worcestershire, and hot sauce; pour into slow cooker. Cover, and cook on LOW 8–10 hours, or until fork-tender.

5) Remove beef tips, cover to keep warm, and set aside.

6) Turn crockpot to HIGH, and cook until gravy thickens. (May also carefully transfer to a saucepan on the stovetop to speed up thickening.) If gravy is not thick enough, combine cornstarch with a small amount of cool water to make a slurry, then whisk into gravy, and bring to a boil. Reduce heat, and simmer until thickened.

7) Return tips to gravy, just to warm through. Serve over rice or noodles.

Barbecue Beef for Sandwiches

Beef for sandwiches with a delicious homemade barbecue sauce is made so easy with a slow cooker. Pop it all in in the morning, and come home to an easy supper.

BEEF & PORK

1 green bell pepper, chopped

1 small yellow onion, chopped

1 (6-ounce) can tomato paste

½ cup packed light brown sugar

¼ cup apple cider vinegar

1 tablespoon chili powder

2 teaspoons kosher salt

1 teaspoon dry mustard

2 teaspoons Worcestershire

Couple dashes hot sauce (optional)

3 pounds braising beef (stew meat, bottom round, chuck)

1) Whisk together all ingredients, except meat, in a slow cooker. Add meat, cover, and cook on HIGH for 7 hours.

2) Shred meat, and pile on toasted buns.

Prep time:	Cook time:	Servings:
10 min	15 min	About 6

Homemade Sloppy Joes

This Homemade Sloppy Joe beats any canned version, hands down.

½ tablespoon cooking oil

1 medium onion, chopped

½ medium green bell pepper, chopped

1 stalk celery, chopped

1 pound ground beef

1 large garlic clove, chopped

1 tablespoon Worcestershire

1 teaspoon Tiger Sauce (optional)

1 (15-ounce) can tomato sauce

¼ cup ketchup

Salt and pepper to taste

6 hamburger buns

2 tablespoons butter, melted

1) In a large skillet, heat oil over medium heat. Add trinity (onion, bell pepper, and celery), and cook until softened.

2) Add ground beef and garlic, and cook until beef is browned, breaking up with a potato masher. Drain off grease, if necessary.

3) Stir in Worcestershire, Tiger Sauce, tomato sauce, and ketchup. Simmer 15 minutes, or until mixture begins to thicken. Add salt and pepper.

4) Brush bun bottoms with melted butter, and toast in separate skillet or on stove-top grill.

5) Serve with baby carrots, baked beans, waffle fries, or potato chips, a side salad, and a pickle.

Pizza Sloppy Joes: Substitute a jar of pizza sauce for tomato sauce, and stir in 3 ounces chopped pepperoni. Spoon meat mixture onto bun bottoms, and place 1 tablespoon shredded mozzarella on each bun. Pass under the broiler to melt cheese, and serve immediately.

Creole Stuffed Bell Peppers

SAUCE:

1 tablespoon butter

¼ cup each: chopped onion, celery, and bell pepper

2 (8-ounce) cans tomato sauce

STUFFED PEPPERS:

4 large green, red, or yellow bell peppers

2 tablespoons finely minced onion

½ tablespoon olive oil

1–2 links spicy Italian sausage, casing removed

1 pound ground beef

2 garlic cloves, minced

1 cup cooked rice

½ teaspoon kosher salt

¼ teaspoon black pepper

¼ teaspoon Cajun seasoning

½ cup water

1 (10-ounce) can diced tomatoes and green chiles, drained

1–2 tablespoons bread crumbs (optional)

Freshly shredded Cheddar cheese or thin slices Velveeta

SAUCE:

1) Melt butter in skillet; add onion, celery, and bell pepper, and sauté over medium heat until tender, about 5 minutes. Stir in tomato sauce; simmer 15 minutes. Remove and set aside.

STUFFED PEPPERS:

1) Preheat oven to 350°. Slice peppers lengthwise, stem to bottom; scrape out seeds and ribs. Parboil pepper halves 5 minutes in boiling water. Drain; set aside.

2) Sauté onion in olive oil until tender; add sausage and beef; brown. Drain; add garlic, and cook 1 minute.

3) Stir in ½ cup Sauce; cook 5 minutes. Stir in rice, salt, pepper, and Cajun seasoning.

4) Pour ½ cup water into 9x13-inch baking dish; place peppers in dish. Scoop beef mixture evenly into each pepper half.

5) Mix tomatoes with remaining Sauce; spoon evenly over filled peppers; sprinkle with bread crumbs, if using. Bake, uncovered, 30–40 minutes, until tender and heated through.

6) Add cheese to top, and return to oven until cheese melts.

Glazed Meatloaf

GLAZE:

½ cup ketchup

1 teaspoon mustard

2 tablespoons brown sugar

MEATLOAF:

2¼ pounds ground sirloin

2 garlic cloves, minced

1 medium sweet or yellow onion, minced

3 green onions, minced

1 stalk celery, minced

½ green bell pepper, minced

4 slices white or whole-wheat bread, torn in chunks and ground

½ cup mushrooms, minced

1 cup chicken broth or stock

1 large egg

1 teaspoon kosher salt

¼ teaspoon black pepper

½ teaspoon Italian seasoning

½ teaspoon Cajun seasoning

Hot sauce to taste

1) For Glaze, combine ketchup, mustard, and brown sugar; stir well. Set aside.

2) Preheat oven to 350°. In a large mixing bowl, combine all Meatloaf ingredients; mix gently, and press lightly into 5x10-inch loaf pan. Place on top rack in oven; place a baking pan on rack below to catch any overflow drippings.

3) Bake 1 hour 30 minutes to 2 hours, or until internal temperature reaches 160°. Brush Glaze onto top of Meatloaf the last 10 minutes of cooking.

4) Allow to rest 5 minutes before slicing. Serve with rice or mashed potatoes, and a green vegetable or side salad.

Variation: Serve the Meatloaf with a brown gravy instead of Glaze.

Million Dollar Baked Spaghetti

1 pound thin spaghetti

½ tablespoon butter

1 (8-ounce) carton sour cream

1 cup cottage cheese

1½ cups shredded mozzarella cheese, divided

½ cup grated Parmesan cheese, divided

3 large eggs, beaten

1 cup chopped onion

½ cup chopped bell pepper

1 tablespoon oil

1 tablespoon minced garlic

1 pound ground beef

½ teaspoon kosher salt

¼ teaspoon black pepper

¼ teaspoon Cajun seasoning

½ teaspoon Italian seasoning

1 (28-ounce) can spaghetti sauce, or equivalent homemade

1 (10-ounce) can diced tomatoes with green chiles, undrained

1 cup shredded Cheddar cheese

1) Break spaghetti noodles into half or thirds, and cook al dente according to package directions. Drain, toss with butter, and set aside to cool slightly.

2) Combine sour cream, cottage cheese, ½ cup mozzarella, ¼ cup Parmesan, and eggs. Add mixture to pasta, and toss. Transfer to buttered 9x13-inch casserole dish.

3) Preheat oven to 350°. Sauté onion and bell pepper in oil until tender, about 4 minutes. Add garlic, and cook 1 minute.

4) Add ground beef; cook, stirring regularly until browned, about 5 minutes. Drain off any excess fat. Add salt, pepper, Cajun seasoning, Italian seasoning, spaghetti sauce, and diced tomatoes with green chiles, and stir to combine.

5) Spoon meat mixture over pasta mixture, and spread to edges of pan. Combine remaining 1 cup mozzarella with Cheddar, and sprinkle evenly on top, then sprinkle with remaining ¼ cup Parmesan.

6) Bake, uncovered, 30–35 minutes, or until bubbly. Let rest 15 minutes before cutting into squares.

Prep time:
10 min

Cook time:
7 hours

Servings:
About 12

Mama's Lasagna

I loved my mama's lasagna, and ricotta is not something she ever used. She made hers with cottage cheese, as I also do. It's an extra special treat when it's made with garden tomatoes, so I always reserve some of my Big Batch Fresh Tomato Meat Sauce to make it.

½ tablespoon olive oil

1 (24-ounce) carton cottage cheese (about 3 cups)

2 large eggs, beaten

½ teaspoon salt

2 pounds shredded mozzarella, divided

6 cups homemade Big Batch Fresh Tomato Meat Sauce (next page) or commercial, divided

1 (10-ounce) package lasagna noodles, cooked

Grated Parmesan cheese to taste

Italian seasoning to taste

Cook's Notes: May add 1 pound cooked ground beef, or a combination of beef and sausage. May substitute very thinly sliced mozzarella for shredded.

1) Preheat oven to 350°. Spread olive oil in bottom of 9x13-inch baking dish; set aside.

2) In a bowl, mix cottage cheese, eggs, and salt.

3) Set aside ½ pound mozzarella cheese and ½ cup meat sauce.

4) Prepare layers with ¼ each: the noodles, meat sauce, cottage cheese mixture, and mozzarella. Repeat for 3 more layers. Cover with foil. Bake 40 minutes, or until hot and bubbly.

5) Spoon reserved ½ cup meat sauce on top, then sprinkle with reserved ½ pound mozzarella, Parmesan, and Italian seasoning. Return to oven, uncovered, 8–10 minutes, or until cheese has melted.

6) Remove, and let rest 15 minutes before slicing.

7) Serve with warm French bread and a mixed garden salad.

Prep time:
15 min

Cook time:
2 hours 30 min

Yield:
About 12 cups

Big Batch Fresh Tomato Meat Sauce

This makes a big batch—enough for a crowd or two delicious meals.

1 tablespoon extra virgin olive oil

2 cups chopped onion

2 tablespoons minced garlic

1 (6-ounce) can tomato paste

8 cups peeled, chopped tomatoes, juices retained

2 pounds ground beef

1 teaspoon Italian seasoning

1 teaspoon dried basil

2 large bay leaves

1 teaspoon kosher salt

½ teaspoon cracked black pepper

1½ tablespoons sugar

1 cup beef broth

3 (8-ounce) cans tomato sauce

2 teaspoons dried parsley

½ teaspoon Cajun seasoning (optional)

1) Heat olive oil in large saucepan over medium heat; add onion; cook until softened.

2) Add garlic; cook another minute, then add tomato paste, stirring constantly, for 5 minutes.

3) Add chopped tomatoes (if canned*, cut in can with kitchen shears) with juices, and bring to a boil; reduce to medium, and cover; simmer 30 minutes, stirring occasionally. Purée with an immersion blender, or leave chunky.

4) Cook ground beef in separate skillet; drain fat, and add to sauce along with Italian seasoning, basil, bay leaves, salt, pepper, and sugar. Stir in beef stock and tomato sauce; bring to a boil, reduce heat, and simmer over medium low, covered, 2 hours or longer.

5) Stir in parsley and Cajun seasoning, if using, and adjust seasonings as needed.

*Cook's Note: Out of season, substitute 1 (28-ounce) can whole, Italian-style tomatoes and 1 (28-ounce) can puréed or crushed tomatoes for the fresh.

Dad's Deep South Spaghetti

I like to toss my spaghetti noodles with a little sauce, then top each serving with more sauce, but my husband likes it better all mixed together. Dad serves his this way, and adds thin slices of andouille sausage. I patterned this version after his.

½ tablespoon olive oil

1 large Vidalia onion, chopped

1 large stalk celery, chopped

2 medium green bell peppers, chopped

2 large garlic cloves

1 pound ground beef

¼ pound andouille sausage, very thinly sliced

4 (15-ounce) cans tomato sauce

1 (15-ounce) can diced tomatoes

1 teaspoon hot sauce

½ cup water

½ tablespoon sugar

1 teaspoon dried Italian seasoning

½ teaspoon Cajun seasoning

2 large bay leaves

½ teaspoon kosher salt, as needed

¼ teaspoon black pepper

1 pound vermicelli or thin spaghetti, broken in half

1) Heat olive oil in a large pot, and sauté onion, celery, and bell peppers until tender, about 4 minutes. Add garlic, and cook 1 minute.

2) Add ground beef; cook and stir until no longer pink. Drain off any excess grease. Add sausage; cook and stir 4 minutes.

3) Stir in tomato sauce, diced tomatoes, hot sauce, water, sugar, Italian seasoning, Cajun seasoning, bay leaves, salt, and pepper. Bring to a boil; reduce heat to low, cover partially, and simmer 1 hour. Discard bay leaves.

4) Cook pasta al dente according to package directions; drain well. Add pasta to sauce, mix well; remove from heat, cover, and let rest 10 minutes before serving.

Inactive time:
1 hour

Cook time:
30 min

Yield:
About 4 pies

Baked Louisiana Meat Pies

1 tablespoon vegetable oil

1 tablespoon butter

½ cup diced onion

¼ cup diced green bell pepper

¼ cup diced red bell pepper

½ cup diced celery

1 tablespoon minced garlic

½ pound lean ground beef

½ pound ground pork

Beef stock or broth, as needed

Kosher salt, freshly ground black
   pepper, and hot sauce to taste

1 large egg

½ tablespoon water

DOUGH:

½ cup vegetable shortening

2½ cups self-rising flour, divided

1 egg yolk

½ cup ice water

1) In a heavy-bottomed sauté pan, heat oil and butter over medium-high heat. Add onion, bell pepper, and celery, and sauté 5 minutes, or until vegetables are softened. During last minute or so, add garlic.

2) Add beef and pork; sauté until no longer pink, and liquid has reduced. Simmer 60 minutes. Add small amounts of broth, as necessary, to prevent sticking. Season with salt, pepper, and hot sauce. Remove from heat, and cool to room temperature.

3) For Dough, cut shortening into 2 cups flour. Stir in egg yolk and ½ cup ice water until Dough is sticky. Turn onto floured surface, and sprinkle remaining flour on top, a little at a time, working it in until dough is smooth.

4) Roll out to ⅛–¼ inch thick; cut into 4–6 inch circles. Evenly distribute filling in center of each round. Wet edges, fold over, and lightly seal with tines of fork. Place pies onto a plate lightly sprinkled with flour, and refrigerate 10 minutes.

5) Preheat oven to 400°. Place pies on a greased cookie sheet or pan. Make a couple of small slits in tops of pies; beat 1 egg with ½ tablespoon water, and brush over each pie. Bake 30 minutes or until golden brown.

BEEF & PORK

Prep time:
5 min

Cook time:
10 hours

Servings:
About 12

Spicy Slow Cooker BBQ Pulled Pork

Nothing can be easier than BBQ pulled pork, cooked in a slow cooker, and shredded for sandwiches.

1 large Vidalia or other sweet onion, sliced

All-Purpose Rub (page 186)

1 (6- to 9-pound) pork shoulder

1½ cups homemade or commercial barbecue sauce

½ cup chicken broth

¼ cup yellow mustard

2 teaspoons hot sauce

Couple dashes liquid smoke (optional)

1) Scatter onion in bottom of 6-quart slow cooker. Apply rub to all sides of roast, and place on top of onion, fat side up.

2) In a separate bowl, whisk together barbecue sauce, broth, mustard, hot sauce, and liquid smoke; pour over and around pork. Cover, and cook on LOW 10 hours, or until pork is cooked through, 160°–170° on instant-read thermometer.

3) Transfer pork to a platter, and let rest 5–10 minutes.

4) Carefully pour sauce from slow cooker into a saucepan, spooning off as much fat as possible. Boil until reduced by half and thickened, stirring regularly.

5) Shred or chop pork, and toss with some sauce; serve remaining sauce on the side.

6) Serve on warmed buns and with coleslaw, if desired.

Pan-Fried Pork Chops

These thin-cut pork chops are dredged in a well-seasoned blend of flour and cornmeal, and pan-fried in a cast-iron skillet. Perfect with succotash and sliced Creole tomatoes.

6 bone-in pork chops, about ¼–½ inch thick

½ cup vegetable oil (about ¼ inch)

1 cup self-rising flour

½ cup cornmeal

¼ teaspoon sugar

¼ teaspoon garlic powder

¼ teaspoon Cajun seasoning

2 teaspoons onion powder

¼ teaspoon kosher salt

½ teaspoon black pepper

1) Rinse pork chops, and drain well. Heat oil in a large cast-iron skillet over medium-high heat. Oil is ready when it shimmers.

2) Whisk together remaining ingredients. Dredge pork chops in flour mixture, shake off excess, and carefully slide pork chops into hot oil, cooking in batches. Don't overcrowd.

3) Fry until browned, 3–5 minutes per side, or until cooked through, depending on thickness of chops. Don't overcook. Transfer to rack placed over a pan to drain; serve immediately.

Smothered Pork Chops in Cream Gravy

Pork chops here are smothered in a cream gravy and dressed with sautéed peppers and onion, and then baked low and slow—though the dish may also be low-simmered on the stovetop.

2 tablespoons olive or cooking oil

4–6 bone-in pork chops

Kosher salt and black pepper to taste

½ large Vidalia or yellow onion, sliced

½ large green bell pepper, sliced

Sprinkling of Cajun seasoning

Butter

½ cup all-purpose flour

2 cups water

2 cups half-and-half or milk

1) Preheat oven to 325°. Heat oil in a large skillet over medium heat. Season pork chops with salt and pepper. Add chops to skillet, and sear on both sides. Remove to a baking pan.

2) Add onion and green pepper to skillet, and sauté until lightly caramelized. Transfer to top of chops; sprinkle with Cajun seasoning.

3) In same skillet, add enough butter to bring drippings to ½ cup. Whisk in flour, a little at a time, until no lumps remain.

4) Combine water and half-and-half, and slowly pour into flour mixture, stirring constantly. Cook and stir 5 minutes. Pour over chops, covering completely.

5) Cover baking pan with foil, and bake 1–1½ hours, or until tender. (May also slow simmer on the stovetop in a covered skillet, checking occasionally to make sure it is not sticking.)

6) Serve over a bed of rice, or with mashed potatoes.

BEEF & PORK

Skillet Pork Chops with Pan Gravy

My husband loves pork chops any way that I fix them, and this is a just a simple skillet recipe that he loves. They're fast and tasty.

1–2 tablespoons cooking oil, divided

4–6 (¾-inch) bone-in, rib pork chops

Salt, pepper, garlic powder, and Cajun seasoning to taste

1 cup chicken or beef broth

½ teaspoon dried rubbed sage

¼ teaspoon dried thyme

¼ teaspoon dried rosemary

Couple dashes of Worcestershire

2 tablespoons butter

1 tablespoon cornstarch

1) Heat ½ tablespoon oil in large skillet over medium high. Season chops on both sides with salt, pepper, garlic powder, and Cajun seasoning. Brown in batches, searing both sides, and adding oil as needed. Transfer chops to plate as they are browned.

2) Whisk together broth, sage, thyme, rosemary, and Worcestershire; add to skillet drippings, and bring to a boil; add butter.

3) Reduce to low, and return chops to skillet, turning to coat. Cover tightly, and simmer 25–30 minutes, or until chops are very tender, turning a few times. Remove chops, and cover loosely to keep warm; set aside.

4) Make a slurry of cornstarch mixed with 1 tablespoon water, and slowly stir into pan drippings, bringing mixture up to a boil. Cook, stirring often, until mixture thickens. Season with additional salt and pepper, if desired

5) Return pork chops to skillet, turn to coat, and warm through. Serve.

Slow Cooker Pork Roast with Vegetables

2 tablespoons olive oil or vegetable oil

1 (4- to 6-pound) boneless Boston butt pork roast

Garlic salt, black pepper, and Cajun seasoning to taste

½ cup water

3 large carrots, scraped and cut into chunks

1 stalk celery, cut into chunks

10 small new red potatoes, scrubbed and cut into quarters

2 (10¾-ounce) cans cream of mushroom soup, or 2½ cups homemade (page 53)

½ teaspoon dried thyme

1 teaspoon dried sage

1 tablespoon cornstarch

1) Heat oil in a stainless steel skillet over medium-high heat. Sprinkle roast with garlic salt, pepper, and Cajun seasoning. Brown on all sides. Remove roast, and set aside.

2) Remove excess fat from juices in skillet, and add water; heat to deglaze, and scrape browned bits from bottom.

3) Add carrots, celery, and potatoes to 6-quart slow cooker. Pour in juices, and sprinkle with additional black pepper. Make a well in center of vegetables, and transfer roast, fat side up, to slow cooker. Smear mushroom soup on top, and sprinkle with thyme and sage.

4) Cover, and cook on HIGH 7–8 hours, or on LOW 9–10 hours, or until fall-apart tender.

5) For gravy, mix together cornstarch with 1 tablespoon water or milk to make a slurry. Use a fat separator to remove fat from slow cooker drippings, and transfer drippings to a large skillet. Bring to a boil, and whisk in slurry; reduce heat to medium, and whisk until mixture thickens and reaches desired consistency.

6) Serve with a side salad or green vegetable, rolls or cornbread, and iced tea for a complete meal.

BEEF & PORK

Prep time:
10 min

Cook time:
2 hour 30 min

Servings:
About 12

Brown Sugar and Mustard Glazed Ham

I cook hams with several different glazes, but this classic glaze of mustard and brown sugar cooked in a Coca-Cola syrup, is my favorite and a southern holiday feature.

1 (6- to 8-pound) fully cooked, shank-end half ham

Whole cloves (optional)

1–2 cups firmly packed light brown sugar, divided

½ cup yellow or Dijon mustard

Sliced pineapple (optional)

Cherries (optional)

½ can Coca-Cola Classic, or any type of non-diet soda

1–2 tablespoons butter

Brown Sugar and Ginger Glaze:
Prepare as directed, except reduce mustard by half and substitute 2 tablespoons lemon juice and 1 tablespoon grated fresh ginger.

1) Preheat oven to 350°. Line a roasting pan with foil for wrapping loosely around ham. Place ham in roasting pan.

2) Score ham in crosshatch pattern, and stud with cloves, if desired. Mix brown sugar with mustard to form a thick paste; smear over entire ham. (If using canned pineapple, you may substitute mustard with pineapple juice.) Add pineapple slices, if desired, and using a toothpick, secure a cherry in center of each slice.

3) Pour cola over ham, and wrap loosely with foil. Bake 18 minutes per pound, or until center of ham reaches 140° on instant-read thermometer, basting occasionally.

4) Remove ham to cutting board, and cool slightly before slicing. Plate ham, and pour pan drippings over top.

5) To make a pan gravy, plate ham and drizzle with a few spoons of drippings. Tent loosely with foil to keep warm. Transfer remaining drippings to a skillet, and bring to a boil; stir in 1–2 tablespoons butter to add richness, and thicken slightly. Place into a gravy boat to pass at the table.

BEEF & PORK

| Prep time: 5 min | Cook time: none | Yield: About 1 cup |

All-Purpose Rub

This is a great all-purpose rub that may be used on all kinds of foods. I love this on steaks, but DeepSouthDish.com readers have used it on ribs, chicken, pork chops, brisket, and even shrimp.

½ cup packed dark brown sugar

1 tablespoon paprika

1 tablespoon chipotle chili powder

1 tablespoon kosher salt

½ tablespoon freshly cracked black pepper

1 tablespoon Cajun seasoning

1 tablespoon garlic powder

1 tablespoon onion powder

1) Mix all rub ingredients with a fork until well combined.

GENERAL USE:

1) Place meat on a glass plate or platter. This recipe will cover 4 (¾-inch thick) beef steaks (NY strip, T-bone, or ribeye).

2) Apply half of rub mixture on one side of meat. Turn, and apply remaining rub on other side, covering all sides. Cover with plastic wrap, and refrigerate several hours or overnight.

3) Bring to room temperature, about 30 minutes. Remove plastic wrap. Grill or pan-fry, as usual; let rest 5 minutes before serving.

BEEF & PORK

Desserts

Prep time:
10 min

Cook time:
1 hour

Servings:
About 8

Classic Southern Pecan Pie

Follow these instructions and tips, and you'll have yourself a perfect Southern Pecan Pie.

3 large eggs

¾ cup sugar

1 cup light corn syrup

2 tablespoons unsalted butter, softened

1 heaping tablespoon all-purpose flour

1 teaspoon vanilla extract

1 cup coarsely chopped pecans

1 (9-inch) unbaked pie shell

1) Preheat oven to 350°. Whisk eggs with sugar; whisk in corn syrup and butter. Mix in flour and vanilla with wooden spoon; fold in pecans.

2) Pour into unbaked pie shell, and bake 55–60 minutes, or until a knife inserted into center comes out clean.

PECAN PIE TIPS:

• Toast pecans for enhanced flavor.

• Don't use a blender or a mixer. Use a whisk and a wooden spoon, and hand mix only—and don't beat it to death! Many pecans pies end up runny due to overbeating.

• Shield edges of pie with foil about halfway through cooking time to prevent over-browning.

• Let pie cool completely before slicing. You should be able to comfortably hold the pie pan flat in the palm of your hand. If it's still too hot to do that, it's too hot to cut!

• Pie is done when a knife inserted into center comes out fairly clean. The filling will still seem a bit jiggly as a whole, but that's normal—it will continue cooking a bit even after removed, so you don't want to overcook it!

Chocolate Pecan Pie: Reduce pecans to ¾ cup, and add ½ cup semisweet chocolate chips with pecans.

Bourbon Pecan Pie: Omit vanilla extract, and add 1 tablespoon of good quality bourbon.

Southern Fried Hand Pies

A true southern classic! In a pinch, I've used canned biscuits in place of homemade Dough with good results. Best served warm, but delicious cold, too!

APPLE FILLING:

½ stick unsalted butter

¼ cup sugar

2 Granny Smith apples, peeled, cored, and chopped (about 2 cups)

1 tablespoon brown sugar

¼ teaspoon ground nutmeg

½ teaspoon ground cinnamon

DOUGH:

½ cup vegetable shortening (like Crisco)

2½ cups self-rising flour, divided

2 tablespoons sugar

Yolk from 1 egg

½ cup ice water

Vegetable oil, for frying

Sugar or powdered sugar

1) For Apple Filling, melt butter and sugar together in large saucepan over medium heat. Add chopped apples, cover, and simmer 15–20 minutes. Remove from heat, and sprinkle brown sugar, nutmeg, and cinnamon over apples; stir, taste, and adjust sweetness. Set aside to cool.

2) For Dough, cut shortening into 2 cups flour. Stir in sugar, egg yolk, and ice water until dough is sticky. Turn out onto a floured surface, and sprinkle more flour on top, working it in until dough is smooth.

3) Roll out to ⅛–¼ inch thick, and cut into 4- to 6-inch circles. Or pinch off golf ball-size pieces, and flatten individually by hand. Place about ½ tablespoon cooled filling in center of each round. Barely wet edges of round with water, fold over, lightly press down on edges; seal with tines of a fork. Place pies in a single layer onto a plate dusted with flour; refrigerate 10 minutes.

4) Fry in a skillet, in about ½ inch of hot oil (at least 350°), until browned on both sides. Remove from skillet, drain on paper towels, and sprinkle with powdered sugar while still warm.

Variations for Southern Fried Hand Pies

To Bake: Make 2 small slits in dough to vent steam, sprinkle with sugar, and bake at 400° on greased cookie sheet for 20 minutes, or until golden brown.

To Use Dried Fruit: Combine 2 (7-ounce) packages dried fruit, 2 cups water, and 1 cup sugar in heavy saucepan. Bring to a boil; reduce heat, and simmer 20 minutes. Add seasonings and proceed.

Peach Filling: Peel and chop 2 pounds ripe peaches. Let drain in colander for 30 minutes, then sprinkle with ¼ cup sugar. It is not necessary to stew, unless you prefer it.

Berry Filling: Add 2 cups fresh berries of choice (strawberries, blackberries, blueberries) to a saucepan; add ¼ cup sugar. Increase sugar as needed. Add 2 teaspoons fresh lemon juice and a pinch of zest. Mix 2 tablespoons cornstarch with 1 tablespoon water, and add to mixture. Bring to a boil, and cook until mixture thickens. Remove and mash berries to desired consistency. Set aside to cool completely.

Sweet Potato Filling: Combine 2 cups cooked, mashed sweet potatoes, with 1 stick softened butter, 1 cup packed light brown sugar, a pinch of salt, and ½ teaspoon each of cinnamon and nutmeg, plus enough milk to moisten. Also can be made with leftover candied yams and sweet potato casserole.

Chocolate Filling: Combine 2 cups sugar with 6 tablespoons cocoa powder. Add 1 stick melted butter.

Prep time:
15 min

Cook time:
1 hour

Servings:
About 6

Old-Fashioned Lemon Meringue Pie

1½ cups sugar

½ cup cornstarch

3 tablespoons all-purpose flour

¼ teaspoon salt

1½ cups boiling water

4 large eggs, separated, reserve whites

2 tablespoons unsalted butter

4 medium lemons, zest and juice

1 (9-inch) pie crust, baked, cooled

MERINGUE:

4 reserved egg whites, room temperature

½ teaspoon cream of tartar

½ cup sugar, or ¼ cup powdered sugar

1) Preheat oven to 350°. In top of double boiler, whisk together sugar, cornstarch, flour, salt, and boiling water. Bring to a boil over medium-high heat, stirring constantly, until mixture begins to thicken, about 10 minutes.

2) Beat egg yolks; temper yolks by beating 1 spoonful hot mixture into yolks at a time, to equal the volume of yolks. Stir tempered eggs into hot mixture.

3) Bring to a boil again, reduce heat to low, and cook 5 minutes, or until very thick.

4) Remove from heat; stir in butter, lemon zest, and juice. Keep warm.

MERINGUE:

1) Beat egg whites on medium speed until frothy. Add cream of tartar and sugar, a little at a time, until incorporated. Increase speed to medium high, beating until stiff.

2) Stir filling, and transfer to baked pie shell. Immediately spread Meringue over hot filling, forming peaks, and spreading to edges to seal.

3) Bake 12–15 minutes, or until peaks are golden brown. Place on a rack to cool, about 2 hours. If possible, refrigerate, uncovered, 8 hours or overnight, before serving. Refrigerate leftovers.

DESSERTS

Prep time:
20 min

Cook time:
50 min

Servings:
About 8

Southern Sweet Potato Pie

1–1½ pounds sweet potatoes, peeled and cubed (about 2 large)

1 cup chopped pecans

¾ cup packed light brown sugar

2 large eggs, separated

¾ cup half-and-half

1 teaspoon vanilla extract

¼ teaspoon ground ginger

½ teaspoon cinnamon

½ teaspoon nutmeg

½ stick butter, softened

Pinch of cream of tartar

1 tablespoon sugar

1 (9-inch) unbaked pie shell

1 tablespoon cane, sorghum, or maple syrup (optional)

Fresh whipped cream

1) Steam or boil cubed sweet potatoes until tender; set aside to cool slightly. Preheat oven to 350°. Toast pecans in skillet until fragrant. Set aside.

2) Put sweet potatoes in a food processor with brown sugar, egg yolks, half-and-half, vanilla, ginger, cinnamon, and nutmeg. Add butter, and process until well blended.

3) In mixer bowl, whip egg whites with cream of tartar until foamy. Add sugar, and beat until stiff peaks form. (You should be able to hold mixing bowl upside down without whipped egg whites sliding out.)

4) Add sweet potato mixture to whipped egg whites until blended well; pour into pie shell. Sprinkle pecans on top, and drizzle with syrup, if desired.

5) Bake 45–50 minutes, or until set. Shield edges with aluminum foil about halfway through cooking to avoid overbrowning.

6) Let cool completely before cutting. Top with fresh whipped cream. Refrigerate any leftovers.

DESSERTS

Simply Superb Peach Cobbler

1 cup self-rising flour

½ cup plus 1 tablespoon granulated sugar

Pinch of salt

1 stick unsalted butter, divided and melted separately

1 (28-ounce) can sliced peaches in heavy syrup

1) Preheat oven to 350°. Butter an 8x8-inch baking dish; set aside. Whisk flour with ½ cup sugar and a pinch of salt. Add ½ stick butter that has been melted; mix with fork until crumbs form.

2) Sprinkle ⅓ crumb mixture into bottom of prepared baking dish. Evenly distribute peaches on top, and pour syrup over. If juices do not nearly cover peaches, add a bit of water to cover. Top peaches with remaining flour mixture. Sprinkle top with remaining tablespoon sugar, and remaining ½ stick melted butter. Bake about 50 minutes, or until bubbly, batter is cooked through and top is lightly browned.

Cook's Notes: Be sure to use self-rising flour, not all-purpose. For fresh, peel and slice 4 large peaches, and sprinkle with an additional ½ cup sugar; refrigerate 2–3 hours before baking. Double for a 9x13-inch dish. (Great served with a scoop of ice cream on top.)

DESSERTS

Prep time: 10 min

Cook time: 25 min

Servings: About 9

Easy Party Cheesecake

CRUST:

1½ cups graham cracker crumbs

1 stick butter, melted

CHEESECAKE:

2 (8-ounce) blocks cream cheese, softened

½ cup sugar

Juice of 1 lemon (about 2 tablespoons)

1 teaspoon vanilla extract

2 large eggs

TOPPING:

1 cup sour cream

3 tablespoons sugar

½ teaspoon vanilla extract

1 (21-ounce) can pie filling of choice

1) For Crust: Preheat oven to 350°. Combine Crust ingredients, and press into 8x8-inch baking pan. Bake about 5 minutes to toast; set aside to cool.

2) For Cheesecake: Using a mixer, beat cream cheese until fluffy, then gradually add in sugar. Slowly blend in lemon juice and vanilla. Add eggs, and mix in on low until smooth. Pour into cooled Crust, and bake at 350° for 25 minutes. Remove, and let rest on a rack while making Topping.

3) For Topping: Combine sour cream, sugar, and vanilla. Spread evenly on top of Cheesecake, and return to oven for 5 minutes. Cool completely, and refrigerate several hours.

4) To serve, spread pie filling over top, or spoon over individual squares.

Cook's Note: May serve topped with fresh fruit, caramel sauce, or pecan praline topping in place of pie filling.

DESSERTS

Prep time: 15 min

Cook time: 30 min

Servings: 10–12

Southern Caramel Cake

3 cups cake flour

3 teaspoons baking powder

½ teaspoon salt

2 sticks unsalted butter, softened

2 cups sugar

4 large eggs, room temperature

1 cup milk, room temperature

1 teaspoon vanilla extract

¾ cup finely chopped toasted pecans (optional)

CARAMEL ICING:

2 cups sugar

1½ teaspoons baking soda

2 tablespoons white corn syrup

½ cup buttermilk

½ cup vegetable shortening

1 stick unsalted butter

1 teaspoon vanilla extract

1) Preheat oven to 350°. Spray bottoms of 3 (9-inch) cake pans with cooking spray, line with parchment paper, and spray pan and paper with nonstick baking spray; set aside.

2) In large bowl, sift together flour, baking powder, and salt; set aside.

3) With mixer, cream butter on medium speed; add sugar, a little at a time, beating well, for about 6 minutes total. Reduce speed to low, and add eggs, one at a time. Alternately add flour mixture and milk, starting and ending with flour. Add vanilla.

4) Divide batter into pans, and level. Bake 25–30 minutes, until toothpick comes out clean, checking at 20 minutes. Don't overcook. Cool in pan 10 minutes, then turn out onto wire rack to cool.

CARAMEL ICING:

1) Combine all icing ingredients, except vanilla, in a saucepan. Cook over medium heat, whisking constantly, until caramel color. Remove from heat, and add vanilla. Using a hand held mixer, beat until cool, and thick enough to spread.

2) Spread between layers, on top, and sides. If desired, sprinkle nuts on top before icing sets.

DESSERTS

Prep time:
15 min

Cook time:
30 min

Servings:
About 12

Basic 1-2-3-4 Yellow Birthday Cake

This made-from-scratch cake, gets its name from the use of 1 cup butter, 2 cups sugar, 3 cups flour, and 4 eggs. In our house, it's traditionally served on birthdays, but great any day!

2 sticks unsalted butter, softened

2 cups sugar

4 large eggs

3 cups sifted self-rising flour

1 cup milk or buttermilk

1 teaspoon vanilla extract

CHOCOLATE BUTTERCREAM ICING:

1 stick unsalted butter, softened

½ cup unsweetened cocoa

1 teaspoon vanilla extract

4–6 tablespoons milk, divided

4 cups powdered sugar, divided

1) Preheat oven to 350°. Butter and flour 3 (9-inch) cake pans, or coat with nonstick baking spray; set aside.

2) In mixer, cream butter until fluffy, then add sugar, beating on high about 8 minutes. Add eggs, one at a time, mixing well after each addition. Alternately add flour and milk, starting and ending with flour. Add vanilla, and mix well.

3) Divide batter into prepared baking pans; bake 25–30 minutes, or until cake begins to draw away from edges, and a toothpick inserted into center comes out clean.

4) Remove from oven, and cool in pans 10 minutes. Turn out on wire rack, and cool completely before frosting.

5) For Icing, cream butter; add cocoa, vanilla, and 4 tablespoons milk, and continue mixing until smooth. Add 3 cups powdered sugar, and continue beating. Add remaining 1 cup powdered sugar, a little at a time, with remaining 1–2 tablespoons milk, adding only enough milk for desired consistency.

DESSERTS

Prep time: 15 min

Cook time: 40 min

Servings: 10–12

Mama's Red Velvet Cake

1 stick unsalted butter, softened

1½ cups sugar

2 large eggs

2 heaping tablespoons cocoa

2 ounces red food coloring

2¼ cups cake flour

½ teaspoon salt

1 cup buttermilk

1 teaspoon vanilla extract

1 tablespoon white vinegar

1 teaspoon baking soda

ICING:

3 tablespoons all-purpose flour

1 cup whole milk

2 sticks unsalted butter, softened to room temperature

1 cup sugar

1 teaspoon vanilla

1½ cups chopped pecans (optional)

1) Preheat oven to 350°. Coat 3 (8-inch) cake pans with nonstick spray, and line with parchment paper.

2) In a mixer bowl, cream butter and sugar; add eggs, one at a time, mixing well. Combine cocoa and food coloring to make a paste; add to butter mixture.

3) In separate bowl, sift flour and salt. Add to butter mixture, ½ cup at a time, alternating with buttermilk. Add vanilla.

4) Combine vinegar and baking soda (will foam a bit). Fold into batter. Divide batter evenly between pans. Bake 25–30 minutes, or until toothpick inserted into center comes out clean.

5) Cool in pans 5 minutes; turn onto a cooling rack to cool completely before frosting.

ICING:

1) In saucepan, whisk flour and milk; cook over medium heat, stirring constantly, until mixture thickens. Set aside to cool.

2) Cream butter and sugar. Stir in milk mixture and vanilla; beat until fluffy. Frost cooled cake. Sprinkle with chopped pecans, if desired.

Prep time:
10 min

Cook time:
1 hour 10 min

Servings:
About 12

Grandma Mac's Southern Pound Cake

In my mind a perfect pound cake like Grandma's is moist, tender, light, fluffy, creamy, and buttery, all at the same time. Grandma Mac used two sticks of butter and one stick of margarine, though I omit the margarine and use only the 2 sticks of butter.

3 cups sifted all-purpose flour

1 teaspoon baking powder

½ teaspoon kosher salt

2 sticks unsalted butter, softened

1 stick margarine, softened,
   or ½ cup vegetable shortening

3 cups sugar

5 large eggs, at room temperature

1 cup whole milk or half-and-half,
   at room temperature

2½ teaspoons vanilla or almond
   extract

2½ teaspoons lemon extract

Cook's Note: When measuring flour for cakes, spoon flour into measuring cup to overflowing, then level off with a knife, rather than scooping measuring cup into flour, which compacts flour, resulting in a dense and dry cake.

1) Preheat oven to 325°. Butter and flour 12-cup Bundt pan, or coat with nonstick baking spray; set aside.

2) Whisk together flour, baking powder, and salt in a bowl; set aside.

3) Beat butter and margarine on medium speed until creamy. Add sugar, ½ cup at a time, and continue beating until mixture becomes fluffy. Add eggs, one a time, blending completely after each addition.

4) Reduce speed to low; add flour mixture, ½ cup at a time, alternately with milk, starting and ending with flour, until fully incorporated. Blend in extracts.

5) Pour batter into prepared pan, smoothing top. Bake 1 hour and 10 minutes, or until toothpick inserted into center comes out clean.

6) Cool in pan on wire rack 15 minutes before turning out onto rack to cool completely.

DESSERTS

Prep time:
10 min

Inactive time:
12 hours

Servings:
8–10

Punch Bowl Strawberry Angel Cake

This easy-to-make dessert looks pretty, too!

1 (8-ounce) package cream cheese, softened

½ cup sugar

Juice of 2 lemons

1 (14-ounce) can sweetened condensed milk

2 (10-ounce) packages frozen sliced strawberries, thawed

1 (8-ounce) container Cool Whip

1 (15-ounce) prepared angel food cake or pound cake, crusts trimmed

1 pound fresh strawberries, sliced (reserve some for garnish)

¼ cup shredded coconut (optional)

¼ cup finely chopped pecans (optional)

1) Beat cream cheese and sugar together until well combined. Add lemon juice and condensed milk; blend. Add thawed strawberries with juices, and combine well. Carefully fold in Cool Whip; set aside.

2) Cut or tear cake into small bite-size pieces.

3) Arrange ingredients in 14-cup trifle bowl or punch bowl, in 3 layers, placing ⅓ the cake pieces on bottom, topping with ⅓ the Cool Whip mixture, then ⅓ the fresh sliced strawberries, and a light sprinkle of the coconut and pecans.

4) Repeat layers until all ingredients are used, and garnish with remaining shredded coconut and chopped pecans.

5) Cover, and refrigerate overnight before serving, and store any leftovers in the fridge. Increase ingredients as needed for a larger trifle bowl.

Cook's Notes: May substitute a second pound of fresh strawberries for frozen. Slice and mix with ¼ cup sugar. Toss and refrigerate 1 hour, stirring occasionally, before using.

DESSERTS

Icebox Cake

This no-bake dessert is great to take along to a potluck, and easy to adapt to many different versions, according to what fruit may be in season.

FILLING:

1 (8-ounce) package cream cheese, softened

1 (14-ounce) can sweetened condensed milk

2 cups milk

1 (4½-ounce) box vanilla or lemon instant pudding mix

1 (8-ounce) tub Cool Whip, divided

CAKE:

2 cups sliced strawberries

1 pint blueberries, rinsed

1 (14.4-ounce) box graham crackers

Chocolate syrup, to garnish

Cook's Notes: Sugar-free or fat-free products work well for this dessert. Also, experiment with different pudding flavors and fruit or chocolate.

FILLING:

1) Beat cream cheese until smooth. Add condensed milk, and blend.

2) In a separate bowl, beat milk and pudding on medium, until thickened, about 2 minutes. Fold into cream cheese mixture with ½ of Cool Whip.

CAKE:

1) Reserve several strawberries and blueberries for later use as garnish.

2) Spread thin layer of Filling in 9x13-inch dish. Add a layer of graham crackers, trimming to fit as needed. Spread with ½ remaining Filling, and top with ½ the sliced strawberries and ½ the blueberries. Repeat layers. Top with last layer of graham crackers, and reserved Cool Whip.

3) Refrigerate at least 4 hours, or preferably overnight, and keep refrigerated until ready to serve.

4) Garnish with reserved strawberries and blueberries; drizzle with chocolate syrup.

DESSERTS

Prep time:
15 min

Cook time:
25 min

Servings:
8–10

Mississippi Mud Cake

1 cup pecan halves

2 tablespoons butter, melted

½ teaspoon kosher salt

1½ cups all-purpose flour

2 cups sugar

¼ teaspoon kosher salt

½ cup unsweetened cocoa

4 large eggs, beaten

½ teaspoon vanilla extract

2 sticks butter, melted and cooled

1 (10.5-ounce) bag mini marshmallows, or 1 (7-ounce) jar marshmallow crème

FROSTING:

1 stick butter

6 tablespoons milk

4 tablespoons unsweetened cocoa

1 (1-pound) box powdered sugar, sifted

1 teaspoon vanilla extract

1) Toss pecans with butter; roast in 375° oven 12–15 minutes. Remove, sprinkle with salt, and cool on plate; coarsely chop.

2) Reduce oven temperature to 350°. Butter a 9x13-inch pan; set aside.

3) Combine flour, sugar, salt, and cocoa. Blend in eggs, vanilla, and butter. Pour into prepared pan; bake 20–25 minutes, or per toothpick test.

4) Remove from oven; while still warm, top with marshmallows. When somewhat melted, carefully spread with spatula.

FROSTING:

1) Melt butter with milk; remove from heat, and whisk in cocoa. Beat in powdered sugar and vanilla with wooden spoon until smooth; pour evenly over marshmallows.

2) Immediately scatter pecans over top; cool completely before cutting into small squares. Refrigerate leftovers.

Oh My Goodness Chocolate Sin

I'm a big fan of layered desserts, and—oh my goodness—this one is simply not safe in the same room with me. It's a decadent and well-loved dessert made with a shortbread pecan crust, and layers of sweetened cream cheese, pudding, and whipped cream.

CRUST:

1 cup all-purpose flour

1 stick unsalted butter, softened

¼ cup finely minced pecans

FIRST LAYER:

1 (8-ounce) package cream
  cheese, softened

1 cup powdered sugar

1 cup Cool Whip or fresh whipped
  cream

SECOND LAYER:

2 (3.9-ounce) packages instant
  chocolate pudding mix

3 cups whole milk

TOPPING:

1–2 cups Cool Whip (or fresh)

Grated chocolate or Heath bits,
  for garnish (optional)

Additional chopped pecans, for
  garnish (optional)

1) For Crust: Preheat oven to 350°. In a bowl, mix together Crust ingredients until mixture resembles cookie dough. Spread into 9x13-inch glass baking dish. Bake 20 minutes, or until lightly browned. Cool completely, about 1 hour.

2) For First Layer: Mix together cream cheese and powdered sugar until well blended. Add Cool Whip, and mix. Spread over cooled Crust.

3) For Second Layer: Whisk together pudding mixes with milk until slightly thickened, about 3 minutes. Carefully spread over First Layer.

4) For Topping: Spread Cool Whip over Second Layer. Cover, and refrigerate 24 hours. Before serving, grate chocolate over top and sprinkle with chopped nuts, if desired. Cut into squares.

DESSERTS

Best Homemade Chocolate Brownies

Our favorite family recipe for years, this homemade brownie recipe produces a chewy brownie with a crusty top—just as a brownie should be. Perfect—just be sure to do everything in order, and make no substitutions!

¾ cup unsweetened cocoa

½ teaspoon baking soda

⅔ cup cooking oil, divided

½ cup boiling water

2 cups sugar

2 large eggs

1½ cups all-purpose flour

1½ teaspoons vanilla extract

¼ teaspoon salt

1 cup chopped walnuts or pecans

1) Preheat oven to 350°. Butter or spray a 9x13-inch baking pan; place a sheet of parchment paper across pan so that there is overhang on both sides to serve as a lift.

2) In a medium-size bowl, stir together cocoa and baking soda. Blend ⅓ cup cooking oil into cocoa until well mixed and shiny. Add boiling water, and stir until mixture thickens.

3) Add sugar, and stir in eggs and remaining ⅓ cup oil, mixing until smooth. Add flour, vanilla, and salt, blending completely. Add nuts; toss.

4) Pour into prepared pan, and bake 30–35 minutes, or until a toothpick inserted in center returns with just a bit of sticky crumbs clinging on it. Do not overcook.

5) Cool in pan about 2 hours; use parchment to lift from pan, and cut into 12 squares. Store in a covered container.

DESSERTS

Prep time:
10 min

Cook time:
25 min

Yield:
24 squares

Hello Dollies

No matter how you layer them, these classic cookie bars are addictive!

1½ cups graham cracker crumbs (about 8 planks)

1 stick butter, melted

1 (14-ounce) can sweetened condensed milk (NOT evaporated milk)

1 cup semisweet chocolate chips

1 cup butterscotch chips

1⅓ cups flaked coconut

1 cup chopped walnuts or pecans

Cook's Note: Peanut butter flavored chips or white chocolate chips may also be substituted for butterscotch flavored chips.

1) Preheat oven to 350°. In small bowl, combine graham cracker crumbs and butter; mix well. Press crumb mixture firmly on bottom of 9x13-inch baking pan.

2) Pour condensed milk evenly over crumb mixture. Layer evenly with remaining ingredients; press down firmly.

3) Bake 25 minutes or until lightly browned. Run a knife around edge of pan while still warm, to loosen. Cool on a wire rack. Chill, if desired, to speed up firming.

4) Cut into 24 bars. Store covered at room temperature or in the refrigerator.

DESSERTS

Prep time: 10 min

Cook time: 7 hours

Servings: About 12

Peanut Butter Cookie Bars

My mama was a cafeteria lady for my first years of elementary school. Because she had to get there so early, I helped out in the kitchen, punching milk cartons and buttering those fabulous homemade rolls before class. These cookie bars were a cafeteria favorite!

1¾ cups all-purpose flour

½ teaspoon baking soda

1 stick unsalted butter

1 cup creamy peanut butter

¾ cup sugar

¼ cup packed light brown sugar

1 large egg

2 teaspoons vanilla extract

1 cup semisweet chocolate chips

2 tablespoons peanut butter

1 cup chopped peanuts (optional)

1) Preheat oven to 350°. In a medium bowl, whisk together flour and baking soda.

2) In a mixer bowl, cream together butter and peanut butter. Add sugar and brown sugar, and blend. Add egg and vanilla, and mix on medium 2 minutes.

3) Add flour mixture to butter mixture, a little at a time, until blended in. Spread in bottom of ungreased 9x13-inch pan, and bake 20–25 minutes; don't overcook. Cool on a rack.

4) Melt together chocolate chips and peanut butter in microwave on HIGH for 45–60 seconds; stir, and repeat at 15-second intervals, stirring each time until completely melted. Spread on top of bar cookies, and set aside to set. Store covered, at room temperature.

Cook's Notes: Easy to double for a potluck or party, using a half-sheet pan. May also use a cookie scoop: drop cookies, flatten, then bake at 350° for 10–12 minutes. Frost with melted chocolate and peanut butter mixture when cool.

Prep time:
10 min

Cook time:
50 min

Yield:
12 squares

Classic Lemon Squares

I love anything made with lemon. Sweet and tart, these are a classic.

CRUST:

2 cups all-purpose flour

½ cup powdered sugar

2 sticks unsalted cold butter, sliced

FILLING:

4 large eggs

2 cups sugar

⅓ cup freshly squeezed lemon juice

¼ cup all-purpose flour

½ teaspoon baking powder

Powdered sugar to sprinkle on top

CRUST:

1) Preheat oven to 350°. Combine flour with powdered sugar. Using a pastry cutter, cut butter into flour mixture until crumbly.

2) Line a lightly greased 9x13-inch baking pan with parchment paper. (Leave extra along edges so you can lift out of pan after it cools.) Press flour-butter mixture into pan, using a bit of flour on your hands. Bake 20–25 minutes, or until lightly browned.

FILLING:

1) Whisk eggs; add sugar and lemon juice, and whisk together.

2) Combine ¼ cup flour with baking powder; whisk into egg mixture. Pour Filling over baked Crust. Bake additional 25 minutes, or until set.

3) Cool completely on a wire rack. Lift out of pan, sift extra powdered sugar over top, and cut into 12 squares or bars.

Cook's Note: Four medium lemons will produce about ½ cup lemon juice and 2 tablespoons zest.

DESSERTS

Oatmeal Chocolate Chip Cookies

Oatmeal cookies, filled with chocolate chips, and a glass of milk, is a delicious way to usher in cooler temperatures.

1 stick unsalted butter, softened

½ cup vegetable shortening

1 cup sugar

1 cup packed light brown sugar

2 large eggs, room temperature

1 teaspoon vanilla extract

1 teaspoon kosher salt

1 teaspoon baking soda

3 cups oatmeal

1¾ cups all-purpose flour

¾ cup semisweet chocolate chips

¼ cup finely minced walnuts or pecans (optional)

1) Preheat oven to 350°. Cream butter and shortening together in mixer until fluffy; mix in both sugars. Add eggs, one a time, until blended in; add vanilla.

2) Using a wooden spoon, mix in salt, baking soda, oatmeal, and flour. Gently stir in chocolate chips and nuts.

3) For a taller, fatter cookie, chill dough about 15 minutes before baking.

4) Spray baking sheet with nonstick baking spray, or line with parchment paper or nonstick foil. Drop dough by tablespoonfuls, and bake one sheet at a time on center rack of oven 10–12 minutes, or until cookies are lightly golden brown around the edges. They will appear underdone. Cool 2–3 minutes on the baking sheet, then remove to a wire rack to cool completely. Once cooled, store in an airtight container.

Prep time:
10 min

Cook time:
12 min

Yield:
2–3 dozen

Old-Fashioned Sugar Cookies

Next to a buttery shortbread cookie, I love a simple sugar cookie. This dough produces a tender, soft and chewy, basic Old-Fashioned Sugar Cookie.

1 cup vegetable shortening

1½ cups sugar, plus additional sugar for sprinkling

2 large eggs

1 teaspoon lemon extract

1 teaspoon vanilla extract

2½ cups all-purpose flour

2 teaspoons baking powder

¼ teaspoon salt

1) Preheat oven to 375°. Cream shortening; add sugar, a little at a time, beating until light and fluffy. Add eggs and extracts; beat well.

2) Combine flour, baking powder, and salt. Add to creamed mixture, and mix well.

3) Using a small scoop or tablespoon, drop dough on greased or parchment paper-lined cookie sheet, and sprinkle lightly with sugar. Bake at 375° for 10–12 minutes or until edges lightly brown.

4) Let cool for a few minutes on pan, then transfer to wire rack to cool completely.

DESSERTS

Prep time: 15 min

Cook time: 10–15 min

Yield: About 5 dozen

Mama's Pecan Finger Cookies

A heritage recipe from my mama's collection, these cookies are known by many names. Mama's recipe is just perfect, and it is the one Christmas cookie above all others in my holiday baking! This is a large batch cookie recipe, and the vanilla extract is straight from Mama's hand, though you may certainly reduce it.

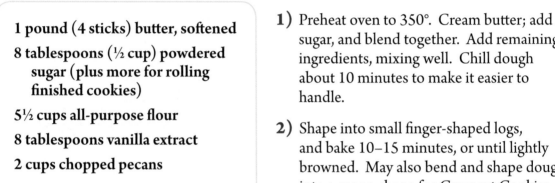

1 pound (4 sticks) butter, softened

8 tablespoons (½ cup) powdered sugar (plus more for rolling finished cookies)

5½ cups all-purpose flour

8 tablespoons vanilla extract

2 cups chopped pecans

1) Preheat oven to 350°. Cream butter; add sugar, and blend together. Add remaining ingredients, mixing well. Chill dough about 10 minutes to make it easier to handle.

2) Shape into small finger-shaped logs, and bake 10–15 minutes, or until lightly browned. May also bend and shape dough into a moon shape for Crescent Cookies, or roll into a ball for Snowball Cookies.

3) Let cool slightly so that you can handle them; but while still warm, roll in the additional powdered sugar to coat; re-roll in the powdered sugar several times, if desired. (I usually roll mine 2 or 3 times.)

4) Set aside to cool completely before storing.

DESSERTS

Prep time:
10 min

Cook time:
8–10 min

Yield:
About 4 dozen

Soothing Snickerdoodles

There's just something about the smell of cinnamon and sugar baking together that is so comforting, and in this world we live in today, we need that.

1½ cups plus 2 tablespoons sugar, divided

2 teaspoons cinnamon

1 stick butter, softened

½ cup vegetable shortening

2 large eggs

2¾ cups all-purpose flour

2 teaspoons cream of tartar

1 teaspoon baking soda

Pinch of kosher salt

1) Preheat oven to 400°. In a small bowl, mix 2 tablespoons sugar with cinnamon; set aside.

2) In a large bowl, cream butter and shortening together; add eggs and remaining 1½ cups sugar.

3) Sift flour, cream of tartar, baking soda, and salt into butter mixture, and blend together.

4) Scoop dough by tablespoonfuls, and roll dough into small balls. Roll dough balls in cinnamon-sugar mixture, and place on ungreased cookie sheet, leaving space between each.

5) Bake 8–10 minutes (depending on how large you rolled the cookies), and transfer from baking sheet to wire rack to cool completely.

DESSERTS

Saltine Cracker Chocolate Toffee Bark

Downright addictive, so super easy to throw together, and made, out of all things, from plain ole saltine crackers, spread with a boiled brown sugar and butter sauce. Semisweet chocolate chips are common for topping, but I love using milk chocolate bars for extra creaminess. These are simply divine!

1 sleeve saltines, or enough to cover a half-sheet jellyroll pan

2 sticks butter

1 cup well-packed light or dark brown sugar

1 (6-pack) full-size Hershey's milk chocolate bars, broken up

⅓ cup crushed pecans or walnuts (optional)

1) Preheat oven to 400°. Line a half-sheet jellyroll pan with foil, turn up edges to form a tray, and spray foil with nonstick cooking spray (or use nonstick foil). Arrange saltines in a single layer with salty side up in lined pan.

2) In saucepan, bring butter and brown sugar to a boil; cook about 3 minutes, stirring constantly. Carefully pour mixture over saltines, and spread evenly, coating each cracker. Bake about 5 minutes until bubbly.

3) While still warm, quickly top crackers with chocolate pieces. As chocolate begins to soften and melt, use a spatula to spread evenly all across top.

4) Sprinkle with chopped nuts. Set aside to cool in the pan, then refrigerate to fully set.

5) Break apart or cut into squares to serve.

Old-Timey Bourbon Balls

1 cup powdered sugar

2 tablespoons cocoa

Pinch of cayenne (optional)

2 tablespoons light corn syrup

¼–⅓ cup bourbon or rum

2 cups crushed vanilla wafers

1 cup finely ground nuts (pecans, almonds, walnuts, or hazelnuts)

COATING: (CHOOSE 1 OR MORE)
- **Finely minced nuts**
- **Sifted powdered sugar**
- **Sifted powdered sugar mixed with cocoa**
- **Finely crushed vanilla wafers or other cookie**
- **Flaked coconut**
- **Melted chocolate or almond bark (chill plain balls 1 hour before dipping)**
- **Drizzle with melted white chocolate or vanilla almond bark**

1) In a large bowl, sift together powdered sugar, cocoa, and cayenne, if using. Stir in corn syrup and bourbon or rum. Add crushed vanilla wafers and nuts; mix well. Dough should be fairly stiff; add more crushed vanilla wafers, if needed.

2) Shape into balls roughly 1 inch in size, and roll balls in Coating.

3) Refrigerate or freeze to set. Serve at room temperature, but store leftovers in the refrigerator.

Variations: Substitute chocolate wafers for vanilla wafers. Add-ins: ¼ cup finely chopped, well-drained maraschino cherries; ¼ cup flaked coconut; 1 teaspoon instant coffee alone, or with 1 tablespoon Kahlúa.

DESSERTS

Prep time:
30 min

Inactive time:
1 hour

Servings:
About 12

Banana Pudding with Meringue

A true southern classic, no event in the Deep South would be complete without somebody bringing a big bowl of banana pudding topped with a fluffy meringue. I make mine in the same bowl that Mama always used, so it feels like a part of her is with me.

¾ **cup sugar, divided**

⅓ **cup all-purpose flour**

Dash of salt

3 cups whole milk

3 large eggs, room temperature, separated

1 overflowing teaspoon vanilla extract

1 box Nilla Vanilla Wafers

4–6 ripe bananas, sliced

Pinch of cream of tartar

Cook's Notes: Double for a potluck or larger casserole dish. I almost always double the custard portion of this recipe. May also place meringue under a broiler with the door cracked for mere seconds, until peaks brown—keep an eye on it.

1) In top of a double boiler, whisk together ½ cup sugar with flour, salt, and milk. Whisk in egg yolks, and cook over medium heat, stirring constantly, until thickened and mixture reaches 170°. Remove from heat, stir in vanilla, and set aside to cool slightly.

2) Preheat oven to 350°. Begin layering in 1½-quart baking dish by spreading a small amount of custard in bottom; add a layer of wafers in bottom; if desired, place wafers around sides of dish with rounded tops facing out. Add ⅓ of the bananas, then ⅓ of the custard. Repeat layers of wafers, bananas, and custard 2 more times to make 3 layers, ending with custard on top. Set aside.

3) Prepare meringue by whipping egg whites with remaining ¼ cup sugar and cream of tartar until stiff peaks form. Spread on top of pudding to edges, making peaks.

4) Bake 15–20 minutes, or until peaks brown.

5) Remove, and let sit at least 1 hour, or refrigerate up to 4 hours before serving. Garnish with a sprinkling of crushed wafers just before serving, if desired.

DESSERTS

Prep time:
15 min

Cook time:
1 hour

Servings:
About 6

Old-Fashioned Southern Bread Pudding

A southern bread pudding using fruit cocktail, and finished with a drizzle of whiskey sauce.

2 tablespoons unsalted butter, melted

1 cup whole milk

1 cup half-and-half

1 (½-pound) loaf French bread, or about 4–5 cups leftover stale biscuits or bread

2 large eggs

1 cup sugar

1 tablespoon vanilla extract

1 (15-ounce) can fruit cocktail, drained

½ cup golden raisins (optional)

WHISKEY SAUCE:

1 stick unsalted butter

¼ cup sugar

½ cup heavy cream or whole milk

1 tablespoon all-purpose flour

½ teaspoon vanilla extract

1 tablespoon bourbon whiskey

Cook's Note: May omit whiskey for a simple glaze, or substitute rum, if desired.

1) Preheat oven to 350°. Coat sides and bottom of 9x9-inch baking dish with melted butter. Set aside.

2) In a large bowl, whisk together milk and half-and-half. Tear bread into small pieces, and place into mixture. Let rest 10 minutes; stir.

3) In a separate bowl, whisk eggs with sugar and vanilla until well blended. Pulse fruit cocktail in a food processor or blender to break it up, but don't purée it. Add fruit cocktail and raisins to egg mixture; pour over bread, and gently mix. Spoon into prepared baking dish.

4) Bake 1 hour, or until bubbly on the sides, golden brown, and set in the middle.

5) Let cool about 5 minutes before cutting.

WHISKEY SAUCE:

1) Melt butter in a saucepan, and whisk together remaining ingredients, except vanilla and whiskey; bring to a boil. Reduce heat, and simmer until thickened.

2) Remove from heat; whisk in vanilla and whiskey, and drizzle over individual servings of warm bread pudding.

DESSERTS

Old-Fashioned Baked Custard

There is something so comforting about this simple old-fashioned egg custard. I like mine with a sprinkling of toasted coconut.

2½ **cups whole milk**

4 **large eggs**

½ **cup sugar**

Pinch of salt

1 **teaspoon vanilla extract**

⅓ **cup sweetened flaked coconut, toasted, divided (optional)**

Whole nutmeg

Boiling water

1) Preheat oven to 325°. Butter 6 small ramekins; set aside. Heat milk to near boiling; set aside.

2) Whisk eggs; beat in sugar, a little at a time. Add salt, and slowly beat in hot milk, a little at a time, so as not to scramble eggs. Add vanilla, and all but 1 tablespoon coconut. Pour evenly into ramekins. Grate nutmeg on top of each.

3) Set ramekins in baking dish, and slowly pour boiling water around them, up to just under the rims, taking care not to allow water to come up over the tops.

4) Bake about 45 minutes, or until knife inserted comes out clean. Remove from oven slowly to avoid splashing water into custards. Using an oven mitt, carefully remove each ramekin from water.

5) Sprinkle reserved 1 tablespoon coconut over top of each custard as a garnish. Let cool slightly, if serving warm; refrigerate, if serving cold.

DESSERTS

Index

Vegetables & Side Dishes

About the Author

Mary is a home cook and the publisher of the wildly popular southern recipe website, DeepSouthDish.com, drawing millions of readers a month from all across the world, who find a reconnection to their own memories and heritage through her childhood stories, and the classic, homespun recipes connected to them.

A multi-generational southerner whose ancestors have found home in at least four southeast states, Mary lives with her husband "The Cajun," and multiple four-legged rescue children, on the Mississippi Gulf Coast, where except for several years living in New Orleans, she has spent her entire life. She is mother to Chris and grandmother to Brian, Sydney and Hugh, each of whom she draws into the kitchen every chance she gets.

Acknowledgments

First and foremost, the glory goes to God. Never once believe that when one door in your life closes, He doesn't already have an even better plan lined up.

To Barney and Gwen, Terresa, Cyndi, and Melinda, who first stumbled across and introduced my blog to the rest of the Quail Ridge Press publishing team, thank you for bringing my blog to life in the pages of a long-sought-after cookbook for my readers, and for putting so much loving care into the process.

To my beautiful mama Helen, you are the inspiration behind this book, and the one who gave me the passion for cooking and sharing food. Through the connection of the Internet, there are now folks all over the world loving our cooking. This would not have happened without the foundation given to me by you. You were the best cook ever, and I'm still trying to make my gumbo taste exactly like yours! It's missing a key ingredient though—you. Heaven got a perfect angel the day you left us.

Grandma Mac, you live on through so many of the recipes I share that I cannot cook them without thinking of you. You would be happy to know that your son James has carried on the pound cake tradition in the family.

To my husband and CEO of tasting—"The Cajun"—thank you for telling me that everything I make is delicious, and for being my number one cheerleader. To Mom and Dad Foreman, thank you for all that you do. You are a treasure and a blessing, and the world is a better place having you in my life. I love you both.

To my brother Mike and my sister Sandra, I miss you both and love you dearly. To you and to the rest of the family, I hope this cookbook brings you joy and a tiny taste of home. To my son Chris, and my daughter-in-law Nikki, thank you for your love and support, for sharing the website with your friends, and helping Deep South Dish to grow. It is your legacy.

To my bright and talented grandson Brian, you were the first, and I am so proud of the young man you are becoming. I can't even express the delight I took when you plucked a stem of parsley from my garden, asked about it, and simply ate it! You might just be the next home chef in the family.

To my beautiful granddaughter Sydney, I will continue to get you in the kitchen to bake every single chance I can. You're a natural at it! The very first KitchenAid I received from your great grandmother is waiting in my pantry for you to treasure in your own home one day.

To my sweet grandson Hugh, your turn is coming. Expect to meet the kitchen just as your brother and sister have.